CITYSPOTS
PARIS

Garry Marchant & Marnie Mitchell

Thomas Cook

KU-444-354

Written by Garry Marchant & Marnie Mitchell
Updated by Aude Pasquier

Published by Thomas Cook Publishing
A division of Thomas Cook Tour Operations Limited
Company registration No: 1450464 England
The Thomas Cook Business Park, 9 Coningsby Road
Peterborough PE3 8SB, United Kingdom
Email: books@thomascook.com, Tel: +44 (0)1733 416477
www.thomascookpublishing.com

Produced by The Content Works Ltd
Aston Court, Kingsmead Business Park, Frederick Place
High Wycombe, Bucks HP11 1LA
www.thecontentworks.com

Series design based on an original concept by Studio 183 Limited

ISBN: 978-1-84157-918-4

Series Editor: Kelly Anne Pipes
Production/DTP: Steven Collins

Printed and bound in Spain by GraphyCems

Cover photography (Sacre-Coeur) © Michel Setboun/Getty Images

CONTENTS

SYMBOLS KEY

The following symbols are used throughout this book:

ⓐ address ☎ telephone ⓕ fax ⓦ website address
🕒 opening times Ⓝ public transport connections ⓘ important

The following symbols are used on the maps:

ⓘ	information office	▢	points of interest
✈	airport	○	city
✚	hospital	○	large town
🛡	police station	○	small town
🚌	bus station	═	motorway
🚆	railway station	—	main road
Ⓜ	metro	—	minor road
✝	cathedral	—	railway
❶	numbers denote featured cafés & restaurants		

Hotels and restaurants are graded by approximate price as follows:
£ budget price ££ mid-range price £££ expensive

Abbreviations used in addresses:
av.   avenue
blvd   boulevard
pl.   place (square)

◐ *The Arc de Triomphe: Napoleon's victories set in stone*

INTRODUCING
Paris

Introduction

The key to Paris's immense attractiveness – and it's the most popular tourist destination on the planet – is its charisma: it knows that, even after all these years, it still sets the standard.

With an almost magnetic beauty, Paris's visual appeal makes it easily the world's most gorgeous city. In the space of a few miles you'll find tree-lined boulevards such as the Champs-Élysées and Saint-Germain, and magnificent monuments such as the Arc de Triomphe, the Louvre and Notre-Dame. Even the town hall, the Hôtel de Ville, is a work of art. And then there are the bridges, the fountains and the Seine itself.

Yet the city has more to offer than good looks; indeed, Paris's record of cultural achievement makes superlatives inevitable. Year after year, it presents the world with the most intriguing museums, the most exciting sense of fashion, the most progressive artistic innovations and, of course, the most ravishing food and drink.

The long-established human iconography of the city – cancan dancers at the Moulin Rouge, accordion players in the metro, booksellers along the Seine – exists in real life to this day, and with a sense of style that prevents any chance of a descent into cliché. Paris isn't self-satisfied, stodgy or staid; it's vibrant, vital and quirky. This is, after all, the city that has the panache to build its own temporary beach once a year so that the people who live and work here can go on holiday every lunchtime; this is the city that has enough sense of fun to turn itself into a giant rollerblading circuit every Friday night when thousands of skaters whizz through its cobbled streets and gigantic thoroughfares; this is the city that sprays perfume all over its underground system in the morning because it allows its homeless to sleep there at night.

Living is considered an art form here, and every reaction to the experience of life is given stylish expression. Religion is practised and celebrated with gusto; so is love, so is art and so are bawdiness and sleaze.

It's so easy to take it all for granted, but imagine what the world would be like without Paris. If the city didn't exist, we'd simply have to invent it. Thankfully, the French already have, and you really should come and make the most of the huge favour they've done the rest of us.

○ *The city's most iconic image*

When to go

Paris is an unsurpassable destination at any time of the year. Summer favours strolling in parks and boulevards, taking a trip on the Seine or spending hours sitting outside a café. Winters are great for investigating the city's cultural and entertainment venues – and for spending hours sitting *inside* a café.

SEASONS & CLIMATE

While Paris is at its most beautiful in spring and autumn, it is worth visiting at any time. Summer can be hot, but it is generally pleasant, with more hours of daylight. In August, quite a few Parisians leave the city for their annual holiday, so many non-central restaurants, cafés and small businesses close.

Tourists descend on the city year-round, but particularly in July and August, so queues at museums and other attractions can be long. During autumn, parks, gardens and tree-lined boulevards are awash with rich colours, and leaves pattern the ground as days get shorter and cooler.

Paris may see the occasional grey day in autumn and winter, but temperatures are rarely extreme.

ANNUAL EVENTS

There is always something going on in Paris, more than even a resident could ever hope to attend. For the latest information on events, see **ⓦ** www.parisinfo.com

January–February

Paris-wide sales last from mid-January to late February. Parisians' sales protocol is considerably less feral than that of their Anglo-Saxon neighbours.

April

Grandes Eaux Musicales (musical fountain displays) Performed on Saturdays, Sundays and some public holidays from April to the start of October. ⓐ Parc du Château de Versailles ⓘ Bookings 01 30 83 78 89 ⓦ www.chateauversailles-spectacles.fr or www.chateauversailles.fr Ⓝ RER: Versailles-Rive Gauche

Marathon de Paris A 42-km (25-mile) race through Paris, starting at the Champs-Élysées (8th). ⓦ www.parismarathon.com

If this is too much to start with, try the Semi Marathon de Paris 21 km (13 miles) in March. If that's too much, simply spectate.

May

French Open Tennis Championships This event is both a grand-slammer in its own right and a great gauge for seeing who's on form for Wimbledon. ⓐ Stade Roland-Garros, 2 av. Gordon-Bennett, 16th ⓘ 01 47 43 48 00 ⓦ www.rolandgarros.com Ⓝ Metro: Porte d'Auteuil

Musique Côté Jardin Music is performed in the city's parks and gardens from May to October.

June–August

Le Cinéma en Plein Air (June & July) A massive screen is set up in the park and, for two months, you can settle in a deckchair and watch late-evening showings of classics as late evening turns into night. ⓐ Parc de la Villette, 19th ⓦ www.villette.com

International Paris Air Show (early June) Chocks away for daring displays of aeronautical expertise. ⓐ Le Bourget Airport ⓦ www.salon-du-bourget.fr or ⓦ www.bourget.epistema.com

Paris Jazz Festival The best jazz sounds are played from early June to the end of July. ⓐ Parc Floral de Paris, 12th ⓘ 01 42 76 47 12 01 46 21 08 37 ⓦ www.parcfloraldeparis.com

Bastille Day (14 July) Celebrate France's national holiday with dances on the 13th, and a parade down the Champs-Élysées with jets and fireworks swooping overhead.

Festival Chopin A celebration of the semi-French composer begins in mid-June and lasts for a month. ⓦ www.frederic-chopin.com ⓘ 01 45 00 22 19

Finale of the Tour de France (late July) The final stage of the world's most exacting cycle race never fails to excite extreme emotions. ⓐ av. des Champs-Élysées, 8th ⓦ www.letour.fr

Paris-Plage (mid-July–mid-August) Quays on both banks of the Seine in the city centre are transformed into a beach, with music, food, sand and palm trees, *boules* and a general party atmosphere. Following the success of this trend-setting event, cities from Berlin to Rome have created their own versions. ⓘ 01 42 76 47 12 ⓦ www.paris.fr

Quartier d'Été Festival (Summer Festival) Music, movies and other happenings throughout Paris from mid-July to early August. ⓦ www.quartierdete.com ⓘ 01 44 94 98 00

Late August–September

Jazz at La Villette Top names and new artists converge at the Parc de la Villette for this music shindig from the end of August to mid-September. ⓐ Parc de la Villette, 19th ⓦ www.villette.com ⓘ 01 44 84 44 84

Nocturnes Splendid sound and light show from late August to mid-September at the château's Bassin de Neptune. ⓐ Parc du Château de Versailles, Versailles ⓦ www.chateauversailles-spectacles.fr

Journées du Patrimoine Normally off-limits buildings such as the Palais de l'Elysée, the President's residence, are opened to the public for the third weekend in September. ⓦ www.jp.culture.fr

Festival d'Automne à Paris (Paris Autumn Festival) This celebrates autumnal events from mid-September to the end of December. ⓣ 01 53 45 17 00 ⓦ www.festival-automne.com

October

Nuit Blanche All night (usually at the beginning of October) you can visit the normally hidden side of nocturnal Paris, revealed through performances, monument visits and installations. ⓣ 01 42 76 47 12 ⓦ www.paris.fr

---

PUBLIC HOLIDAYS

New Year's Day 1 January
Easter 23–4 March 2008, 12–13 April 2009
May Day 1 May
Victory Day, WW II 8 May
Ascension Thursday 1 May 2008, 21 May 2009
Bastille Day 14 July
Assumption of the Virgin Mary 15 August
All Saints Day 1 November
1918 Armistice Day 11 November
Christmas Day 25 December

Paris: seriously romantic

The marketing of major cities as tourist destinations has long relied on clichés to identify individual brands. Thus New York is a big apple that's so good they named it twice; Copenhagen is wonderful, wonderful; and Rome, Venice and Adelaide are all the one and only City of Light.

And Paris? Is it really, as we are so often told, the city of romance?

Well, it's certainly heaving heaving with amorous couples, romantic alleys and dreamy squares, chief among which is the glorious Place des Vosges in the Marais (see page 44). From the moment this perfectly symmetrical square was completed in 1612, it became a location for romantic couplings, not least thanks to the huge contribution made by its most famous early resident, the prolific courtesan Marion Delorme. Even now, the Town Hall regularly makes the dramatic gesture of filling the square entirely with lavender. So, yes, Paris is romantic, but its residents are hardly coy. André Malraux, the leading French cultural figure of the last century, called the beautiful triangular garden of **Place Delphine** (Île de la Cité, 1st Metro: Cité) 'undoubtedly Paris's vagina'. This was meant as a compliment.

Paris not only deserves its reputation as being literally romantic; it has an irrefutable claim to being literarily Romantic, which is how it acquired its reputation for inspiring a kind of dark and brooding passion (see Paris in the Movies, page 58). The Romantic writers of the 18th century took the Renaissance identification of genius with melancholy a step further by equating it with early death. An international style of conspicuous suffering became popular, and the 1830s saw a rash of 'Suicide Clubs' forming throughout the city. Their members took to hurling themselves into the Seine with such enthusiasm that the clubs were banned. Although this is an idea that today seems risible to all but the most vapid emo who's been plunged into morbid depression by the side effects of his acne medication, Paris has been the site of some iconic premature departures: Oscar Wilde, Jim Morrison and Princess Diana all checked out rather too early here.

Should either the hearts-and-flowers or the deep-and-meaningful facets of Paris's romantic appeal move you to the kind of gesture that can only be made on one knee, another charming square, **Place Vendôme** (ⓐ 1st ⓝ Metro: Tuileries) is full of expensive jewellery shops. And when you've sobered up and realised how much you spent on the ring, a call to the Counseling Centre, an English-language helpline (ⓣ 01 47 23 61 13), should dissuade you from leaping into the river.

◯ *Paris as in the movies...*

History

The French capital began its life as a modest fishing village on a small island (now the Île de la Cité) in the Seine. Around 225 BC, a Gallic tribe, the Parisii, inhabited it, but when Caesar's legions invaded 200 years later, they set fire to their tiny settlement and fled. The Romans subsequently expanded and developed the village, which was just an anonymous outpost of their empire, changing its name first to Lutetia, and then finally Paris.

It was Clovis the Franc who first raised Paris's profile by making it the capital of his kingdom in 470. The city rapidly became a centre of Christianity and remained relatively stable, despite the attentions of the Vikings. The 13th-century reign of Philippe Auguste saw it modernise and expand again; the early Middle Ages were a golden time that only came to an end when Paris was devastated by Black Death. In the late 16th century, Henri of Navarre rebuilt the capital and, by the time Louis XIV (the 'Sun King') came to the throne a century later, it was re-established as an important and sophisticated city. The two subsequent Kings Louis enjoyed their power rather too much, though: during the French Revolution, Paris was absolutely at the centre of events, with the storming of the Bastille prison and a great deal of blood shed on its streets, especially via the guillotine in Place de la Concorde.

Republican Paris developed steadily through the Industrial Revolution, the French Second Empire, and the belle époque. The architectural style by which we identify the city today was established when Napoleon III commissioned Baron Haussmann to transform it into a glorious, 19th-century capital. The Baron largely created the shape of modern Paris, with its broad boulevards and distinctive buildings.

In the 19th and 20th centuries, Paris was enduring the ravages of wars at the same time as it was establishing itself as a centre of artistic achievement and the spicier types of leisure pursuit. Times could be exceedingly hard for Parisians: during the Franco-Prussian War siege, for example, starvation forced them to eat the zoo animals. The city's lowest point in modern history came during World War II, when German troops occupied it for four years.

Charles de Gaulle was the dominant figure in post-World War II France. By May 1968, however, the country had had enough of his system of government (the 'Fifth Republic', which was basically an elected monarchy), and students on Paris's Left Bank started an uprising that eventually led to his downfall. After the uneventful presidencies of Pompidou and Giscard d'Estaing, Mitterrand revived the notion of President as monarch and left behind such monuments to his rule as the Louvre Pyramid and the Opéra Bastille.

His successor, Jacques Chirac, also conducted himself as an autocrat and, although Paris briefly became the focus of the world's attention when Princess Diana was killed in a car crash here in 1997, it is the reaction to Chirac's presidency that has had the largest impact on the feeling of the modern city. While the country as a whole saw a shift to the far right, Paris's impulse was to elect the left-winger Bertrand Delanoë as its Mayor; Delanoë has had a huge impact on the city. Chirac has gone, having been replaced by Nicolas Sarkozy in May 2007, but Delanoë continues as Mayor and has recently unveiled his 'Plan Local d'Urbanisme', a vision of Paris's future that places the income generated by tourism at the heart of the city's economic prosperity. Visitors, then, should look forward to the coming years with anticipation.

Lifestyle

For all its world-renowned monuments, Paris is not a museum but a living city. The Place du Palais Royal, across from the Louvre, is often buzzing with activity, whether it's skateboarders weaving around coloured cones, rap or rock musicians jamming, or a farmers' market selling *pain de campagne* (rustic bread) or *saucisson* (sausage). In many neighbourhoods, food markets are held on weekends,

● *The enjoyable process of becoming café-cultured*

when Parisians patronise their local stalls. (See Ⓦ www.paris.fr for the market list.)

Parisians love to gather at cafés, squares and along the quays and pedestrian bridges (such as the Pont des Arts), whenever time and weather permit. To return central Paris to the people, the City Council closes the Seine-side roads to traffic and opens them to pedestrians on Sundays and public holidays. The result is a huge success, with strollers, cyclists and skaters taking over the riverbanks. On Sundays along the newly popular Canal St-Martin in the 10th *arrondissement*, the quai de Valmy and quai de Jemmapes are also turned over to pedestrians. The Place de l'Hôtel de Ville, in front of the town hall, throbs with activity year-round. In summer, sand and palm trees are transported here for public volleyball courts during the hugely successful Paris-Plage (see page 10) when the quays of the centre are turned into a riverside 'beach'. In the winter, the square transforms into an ice rink, with free skate hire and festive music. The latest ice rink of note, and a huge hit with the locals in winter, is 57 m (188 ft) above ground on the first level of the Eiffel Tower. On fine days, Parisians can be seen walking their dogs or occupying every inch of space on lawns and metal chairs in such parks as the Jardin du Luxembourg (see page 100) and the Jardin des Tuileries (see pages 64–7). Whatever the weather, locals love getting together with family and friends, and young people and couples linger for hours at street cafés, cell phones in one hand, cigarettes in another. However, since 1 January 2008, it is illegal to smoke in all public places, a legislative development that severely tests the rebellious Parisian psyche.

Culture

Paris defines the notion of a cultural city. It has always been a centre of architectural innovation: both the Eiffel Tower and, more recently, I M Pei's glass *Pyramid* at the Louvre, sparked controversy when they were first built, yet today they are heralded as marvels of innovative, cutting-edge design.

Though it was first developed some 30 years ago, the Centre Pompidou (see page 86), which houses the Museum of Modern Art, is still considered revolutionary, which is far from a pejorative term in the local context. Despite the view of some Parisians that the chunky exterior pipes are worthy of a plumber's nightmare, the building is a success for its museum space and panoramic views across Paris.

Another example of original design lies beneath the Eiffel Tower. The Musée du Quai Branly (see page 111), designed by Jean Nouvel and opened in 2006, has a principal façade that follows the curve of the Seine, as well as a 'living culture' space for theatre, music and dance.

As one of the world's cultural capitals, Paris always has exhibitions of such great artists as Ingres, Chagall and Monet; but springing up in the northern Marais neighbourhood is a wonderful collection of small, unpretentious, designer boutiques and art galleries. Among the new, young fashion designers are Gaspard Yurkievich, with a boutique and showroom on 43 rue Charlot, and the boutique, **Shine** (ⓐ 15 rue Poitu, 3rd ❶ 01 48 05 80 10), nearby. The Marais also houses fresh new galleries of contemporary art such as Chantal Croussel, Denise René and Frédéric Giroux (all on rue Charlot).

Even for locals, the choice in Paris can be overwhelming, with some 1,800 classified monuments, 140 museums and 145 theatres.

❶ *Getting to grips with the city's statuary*

The weekly publication *Pariscope* has complete event listings, with around 50 pages dedicated to theatres alone.

The city's museums range from the great, such as the Louvre (see pages 68–9) and the Musée d'Orsay (see pages 109–11), to the offbeat, such as the **Musée de l'Erotisme** (ⓐ 7 blvd de Clichy, 18th ⓣ 01 42 58 28 73) and the **Musée de la Contrefaçon** (ⓐ 16 rue de la Faisanderie, 16th ⓣ 01 56 26 14 00), the latter boasting a fascinating collection of counterfeit objects, from food to perfumes. Freshly opened are the Musée d'Art Moderne de la Ville de Paris (see page 71) on avenue du President Wilson in the 16th *arrondissement*, and the Musée de l'Orangerie (see pages 64–7) in the Tuileries in the 1st.

The two opera houses, the majestic Palais Garnier (see pages 72–3) with its gold leaf embellishments and the modern glass-fronted Opéra Bastille (see page 85), opened for the bicentennial of the French Revolution, provide a full and varied programme of opera and ballet throughout the year (except August, when Paris goes on holiday). In an effort to get younger audiences to attend operatic and ballet performances, the Opéra Bastille has installed 62 standing places, for just €5 per performance, purchased with cash or credit card at ticket-issuing machines. This has been so successful that the same system will soon be installed at the Garnier.

Performing arts venues range from the mega, such as the **Palais des Congrès** (ⓐ 4 blvd des Palais, 6th ⓣ 01 44 32 51 51), to the mini of the cloakroom-sized cabarets and theatres in Montmartre.

Even the quality of the busker is higher in Paris than in many cities, with some highly talented artistes adorning the city's streets and metro stations.

▶ *Just one of the city's spectacular views*

Shopping

Paris is the epicentre of haute couture, with all the top names occupying select addresses along the avenue Montaigne, Champs-Élysées, Faubourg Saint-Honoré and rue Saint-Honoré, Place Vendôme and rue Royale. Even if you can only afford to window shop, it is fun to stroll past such bastions of high fashion as Cartier, Chanel, Louis Vuitton, Gucci, Dior, Lalique, Longchamps, Hermès, Christian Lacroix, Jean-Paul Gaultier and Versace. There is even a list of officially sanctioned haute couture houses at Ⓦ www.modeaparis.com

You can get a cross-section of goods in the city's excellent department stores, such as Galeries Lafayette (see pages 75–6) and Le Printemps (see page 76) on boulevard Haussmann in the 9th *arrondissement*, Le Bon Marché (see page 112), with its famous food store, in the 7th, and the **BHV** (ⓐ 52 rue de Rivoli, 4th ⓣ 01 42 74 90 00), across from the Hôtel de Ville in the 4th. All have the latest in ready-to-wear fashions as well as household items.

Metrosexuals have their own outlets in such venues as **Madelios** (ⓐ 23 blvd Madeleine, 1st ⓣ 01 53 45 00 00), near the Place de la Madeleine, which features such men's brands as Hugo Boss and Cerruti Jeans. Likewise, Le Printemps has a separate building devoted to menswear.

The Marais, the city's oldest district, where ancient buildings lean into cobbled streets, has an eclectic variety of little boutiques. Although Sunday shopping is largely prohibited except at Christmas time and during the sales (at the end of January and June), it carries on in the Marais (mainly in the 4th), where, on sombre Sundays, busy shops add welcome animation to such streets as Francs Bourgeois and to the Canal St-Martin district in the 10th *arrondissement*. Here,

USEFUL SHOPPING PHRASES

What time do the shops open/close?
A quelle heure ouvrent/ferment les magasins?
Ah kehlur oovr/fehrm leh mahgazhang?

How much is this?
C'est combien?
Cey combyahng?

Can I try this on?
Puis-je essayer ceci?
Pweezh ehssayeh cerssee?

My size is...
Ma taille (clothes)/
Ma pointure (shoes) est ...
*Mah tie/mah
pooahngtewr ay ...*

I'll take this one, thank you
Je prends celui-ci/
celle-ci merci
*Zher prahng serlweesi/
sehlsee mehrsee*

branché (trendy) boutiques around the quays (Valmy and Jemmapes) and side streets also evade Sunday closing.

Across the river on the Left Bank, boulevard Saint-Germain is the thoroughfare to shop, sip coffee, stroll and people-watch. As well as the boulevard itself, its side streets, rue du Four and rue des Saint-Pères, and the streets around St Sulpice church are full of little boutiques selling such items as daring lingerie and funky embroidered bags.

Also not to be missed are the city's many markets, specialising in everything from farm-produced cheeses to *grand-mère's* antiques.

For a stylish memento of your stay, the museum boutiques, selling art cards, prints and classy trinkets, are worth a browse.

Eating & drinking

As a world culinary capital, Paris has an impressive variety of restaurants, brasseries and bistros. With 10,000 bars and restaurants, the only problem you'll have is choosing where to go. Dedicated gourmets can dine at the *crème de la crème*, the chefs' restaurants such as **Fogón** (Spanish cuisine) (🖈 quai des Grande-Augustins, 6th ❶ 01 43 54 82 62 Ⓜ Metro: St-Michel) and **Chez L'ami Jean** (Basque cuisine) (🖈 27 rue Malar, 7th ❶ 01 47 05 86 89 Ⓜ Metro: Invalides). You can chew with a view at the Michelin-rated 2-star **La Tour d'Argent** (🖈 15–17 quai de la Tournelle, 5th ❶ 01 43 54 23 31 Ⓦ www.tourdargent.com Ⓛ closed Mon Ⓜ Metro: Cardinal Lemoine) and the Philippe Starck-designed **Kong** (🖈 1 rue du Pont Neuf, 1st ❶ 01 40 39 09 00 🖈 Metro: Pont-Neuf), where views are superb and lofty, and prices are pretty rarefied, too. ❶ Reservations are essential at each of these restaurants.

A recent trend has seen renowned chefs opening small *prix d'amis* (affordable price) restaurants to bring fine food to a wider group of discerning diners: Alain Senderens renounced his three Michelin stars to set up the unpretentious **Senderens** (🖈 9 pl. de la Madeleine, 8th ❶ 01 42 65 22 90); Pierre Gagnaire opened the **Gaya** (🖈 32 rue Faubourg St Antoine, 12th ❶ 01 43 41 04 10) and others are following suit.

For those on a budget, many restaurants serve set meals of several courses, with *entrée* and *plat* (main course), or *plat* and *dessert*, or all

PRICE CATEGORIES

Restaurant ratings in this book are based on the average price of a three-course dinner without drinks:

£ up to €30   ££ €30–€50   £££ over €50

three for a fixed price. Bistros offer home-style cooking in an informal atmosphere, while brasseries provide sandwiches, salads or simple meals most of the day. Wine bars have quality wines with tasty snacks or meals to accompany them.

Too many simple restaurants and brasseries, especially in tourist areas, limit their menus to roast chicken or steak and chips. If you'd like something other than chips, they may provide a salad or vegetables instead. Despite their modest surroundings and prices, many brasseries and bistros serve fresh market produce.

Eating places are found throughout the city, and often those away from the main tourist sites are of better value and quality.

The greatest collection of budget restaurants is in the popular and touristy Saint-Michel area in the Latin Quarter. The warren of cobbled streets near place Saint-Michel, especially along rues Huchette, Harpe and St-Severin, is crammed with little restaurants and bars. Most prices are low and while quality is not quite haute, some of these places serve very reasonable meals.

The Montmartre area is known for its African restaurants, serving such dishes as *mafé* (West African meat in peanut sauce) and *yassa* (Senegalese chicken, mutton or fish in a lemon, mustard and onion sauce). Chinese fare is authentic and plentiful in the 13th *arrondissement*, Japanese along rue St-Anne in the 2nd,

◆ *A restaurant on the Left Bank*

while Indian restaurants can be found in passage Brady in the 10th. *Traiteurs* (take-aways), especially Chinese, serve budget meals and sometimes you can eat on the premises. They are simple, but good value. (For more info on ethnic food, see Multicultural Paris, pages 118–19.)

French fare changes with the seasons. In autumn and winter, fishmongers set up stalls in front of many brasseries and serve fresh oysters. During cold months, hearty, warming cheese dishes from the mountain region of the Savoy – fondues, *raclettes* and *tartiflettes* – are popular. In summer, fresh fruits and vegetables are plentiful in markets and on menus and Parisians love dining al fresco late into the evening.

It is advisable to book ahead for any of the grand establishments, but it is not necessary for simple restaurants or brasseries, which, unless they are the trendiest places, can be booked on the day you wish to visit. More time should be allowed for reserving at haute cuisine restaurants, which often need to be booked weeks in advance and confirmed the day before. At the more exclusive restaurants, men should wear a jacket and tie, especially in the evenings. Otherwise, the dress code is fairly relaxed. Many restaurants are closed on Sunday, but the local weekly listings publication, *Pariscope*, lists some venues that are open (*ouvert le dimanche*).

Few of France's top restaurants and traditional brasseries are vegetarian-friendly, though some simple cafés, takeaways and lunch

DINING TIPS

In many restaurants dishes are half price at lunchtime, so locals often eat out in the middle of the day.

A 15 per cent service charge is included in the bill, but you can round it up at your discretion.

counters are starting to serve *bio* (organic) fare. One, started by two chefs and known for its quality, is **Eatme** (Ⓦ www.eatme.fr). The dishes served here are approved by a nutritionist.

USEFUL DINING PHRASES

I would like a table for two/three/four people
Je voudrais une table pour deux/trois/quatre personnes
Zher voodray ewn tabl poor dur/ trwah/ kahtr pehrson

Waiter/waitress!	**May I have the bill, please?**
Monsieur/Mademoiselle,	L'addition, s'il vous plaît!
s'il vous plaît!	*Laddyssyawng, sylvooplay!*
M'sewr/madmwahzel, sylvooplay!	

Could I have it well-cooked/medium/rare please?
Je le voudrais bien cuit/à point/saignant s'il vous plaît
Zher ler voodray beeang kwee/ah pwang/saynyang sylvooplay

I am a vegetarian. Does this contain meat?
Je suis végétarien (végétarienne).
Est-ce que ce plat contient de la viande?
Zher swee vehzhehtarianhg (vehzhehtarien).
Essker ser plah kontyang der lah veeahngd?

Where is the toilet (restroom) please?
Où sont les toilettes, s'il vous plaît?
Oo sawng leh twahlaitt, sylvooplay?

Entertainment & nightlife

From all-night discos to cosy wine bars and what some euphemistically call 'naughty Paris', the city truly has something for every nightlife temperament. Whether your aim is to relax, have fun or *se cultiver* (get cultured), there is no lack of choice.

The long summer nights give Parisians several more hours of daylight after their work day, when they can dine or drink at outdoor restaurants and bars. Free summer concerts fill the parks and gardens from May to September, while festivals and music fêtes fill the streets and bars with a lively, late-night atmosphere during sultry months.

Trendy clubs include Rex Club (see page 79), **Le Pulp** (Ⓦ www.pulp-paris.com) and **Le Triptyque** (Ⓦ www.letriptyque.com) in the 2nd *arrondissement*, or **Le Nouveau Casino** (Ⓦ www.nouveaucasino.net) in the hip nightlife district of rue Oberkampf in the 11th. The Bastille district (also in the 11th) is ever-popular thanks to its party atmosphere, bistros, clubs and bars.

The river after dark is as bright with action as it is with lights, aided by such floating clubs as Le Batofar (see page 117) and **The Cabaret Pirate** (Ⓦ www.guinguettepirate.com) in the 13th *arrondissement* and the Bâteau Six-Huit on quai Montebello in the 5th (see page 117). The river clubs offer the best in electro, house and rhythm-and-blues. Another waterside district that has become fashionable is the Canal St-Martin in the 10th, its quays (Valmy and Jemmapes) and side streets buzzing with interesting restaurants and bars.

Jazz-lovers head for the numerous clubs on rue des Lombards near Les Halles and the famous Caveau de la Huchette (see page 117) on the street of the same name in the Saint-Michel district.

Paris has some 100 dance clubs, so there's something for every music taste, from rock, rap, hip-hop and techno to African rhythms,

⬤ *Rue de la Huchette is full of restaurants, bars, clubs and late-night crowds*

salsa and samba. Those who like to party all night long should ask bartenders or party-hearty Parisians where the 'after' bars, often unadvertised, are. Many are in the lively Pigalle area of Montmartre.

In a country synonymous with fine wine, wine bars or quiet places to *boire un verre* (have a drink) are plentiful and varied.

The major museums have at least one late-night opening for culture vultures, while the Opéra National de Paris stages the best of opera and ballet performances at its sumptuous Palais Garnier (see page 72) and its modern Opéra Bastille (see page 85) known for its daring productions.

If just vegging out and seeing the latest Hollywood or French film is your thing, Paris has all the major films in *version originale* (VO) in cinemas at such central locations as the 6th *arrondissement*, the Champs-Élysées, Les Halles and Montparnasse.

Scantily-clad cancan girls in cabaret-type performances strut their stuff in **Le Lido** (📧 116 bis av. des Champs-Élysées, 8th ☎ 01 40 76 56 10), **Le Moulin Rouge** (📧 82 blvd de Clichy, 18th ☎ 01 53 09 82 82) and **Le Crazy Horse** (📧 12 av. George V, 8th ☎ 01 47 23 32 32), among others. The weekly *Pariscope* or *l'Officiel des Spectacles*, available at news-stands, list the full spectrum of more serious eroticism. These two publications also provide up-to-date listings (only in French) of movies, live theatre, exhibitions, sporting events, guided tours and even restaurants.

The main area for gay nightlife is the Marais, though the traditional clubbing focal point is the **Queen** nightclub on the Champs-Élysées (📧 102 av. des Champs-Élysées, 8th ☎ 01 53 89 08 90).

◀ *The legendary Moulin Rouge still operates as an entertainment venue*

Sport & relaxation

SPECTATOR SPORTS
Football & rugby

Fans can see professional football and rugby matches either at the Stade de France or the smaller Parc des Princes, the home stadium of the local football team, Paris Saint-Germain.

Parc des Princes ❸ 24 rue du Commandant Guilbaud, 16th ❶ 01 47 43 71 71 Ⓜ Metro: Porte de Saint-Cloud

Stade de France ❸ 93216 Saint-Denis la Plaine ❶ 0892 700 900 Ⓦ www.stadefrance.fr Ⓝ RER: Stade de France

Horse racing

The main courses are the Hippodrome Longchamp and the Hippodrome d'Auteuil (both in the Bois de Boulogne). For information on all venues, see Ⓦ www3.france-galop.com

Hippodrome d'Auteuil ❸ Butte Mortemart, route des Lacs, 16th ❶ 01 40 71 47 47 Ⓜ Metro: Porte d'Auteuil

Hippodrome Longchamp ❸ route des Tribunes, 16th ❶ 01 44 30 75 00 Ⓜ Metro: Porte d'Auteuil

Tennis

The Roland-Garros stadium is the home of the French Open.

Stade Roland-Garros ❸ 2 av. Gordon-Bennett, 16th ❶ 01 47 43 48 00 Ⓦ www.rolandgarros.com Ⓜ Metro: Porte d'Auteuil

PARTICIPATION SPORTS
Bicycling

Bicycling is a popular, convenient recreation in this city with more than 100 km (62 miles) of cycle lanes. Tourist information offices and bicycle rental shops provide free leaflets detailing routes.

Jogging

Joggers can follow the Seine either down by the riverside or along the streets above. They can also run in and around larger parks such as the Jardin du Luxembourg (see page 100). The Jardin des Tuileries (see page 64) has a jogging trail.

Rollerblading

Paris is a world capital of rollerblading. More than 4,000 skaters hit the streets every week for the Friday night skate-athon. This is open to all, but participants should be reasonably proficient. Beginners should choose the gentler Sunday afternoon events that leave from outside Nomades. The 20-km (12 1/2-mile), three-hour circuit starts at 14.30 from Place de la Bastille. Skates are available to buy or rent at:

Ilios ⓐ 4 allée Vivaldi, 12th ⓣ 01 44 74 75 76 Ⓜ Metro: Daumesnil

Nomades ⓐ 37 blvd Bourdon, 4th ⓣ 01 44 54 07 44
Ⓦ www.nomadeshop.com Ⓜ Metro: Bastille

RELAXATION

Hammams

France's links with Morocco have resulted in Paris being well off for hammams, where a session in a steam room-cum-sauna is the prelude to a vigorous exfoliation (*gommage*) and massage. Thereafter: bliss. Two of the very best are:

Les Bains du Marais ⓐ 33 rue des Blancs-Manteaux, 4th ⓣ 01 44 61 02 02
Ⓦ www.lesbainsdumarais.com Ⓜ Metro: Archives

Hammam Med Centre ⓐ 43 rue Petit, 19th ⓣ 01 42 02 31 05
Ⓦ www.hammammed.com Ⓜ RER: Ourcq

Accommodation

Although international lodging chains are here, most Paris hotels are small, independent establishments. Rooms are often small and lifts can be rickety or nonexistent, but generally these hotels have distinct, charming atmospheres. Service can range from surly to warm and accommodating.

Paris also has a great variety of good mid-range, boutique hostelries, with the most attractive called *hôtels de charme*. Many are set in stately old residences, former monasteries, even churches. What these lodgings lack in space, they make up for in character and personal service. Many have been renovated in recent years, so have modern bathrooms and facilities such as satellite TV and internet and fax connections.

All 2-star hotels and above must have staff competent in at least one foreign language, usually English. Reserve as soon as possible, by email or telephone. Internet booking is becoming increasingly popular, with even the small hotels. All hotels post their rates at the entrance and visitors can walk in off the street to book a room, but this is not advisable during holiday seasons.

In the budget category, with an average rate of €83, Paris is the third-least expensive city in Europe, after Budapest and Frankfurt, according to a survey commissioned by the tourist board.

PRICE CATEGORIES
Accommodation ratings are based on the average price of a double room per night, including breakfast:
£ up to €100   ££ €100–€200   £££ over €200

⬥ *A typical hotel façade in Paris with intricate wrought-iron balconies*

The Paris Visitors Bureau's excellent website is a good central booking site: Ⓦ www.parisinfo.com. Also try Ⓦ www.hotels-paris.com

Below is just a small sampling of the 1,449 hotels in Paris, with special emphasis on those with unique characters or histories.

RIGHT BANK WEST

New Orient Hotel £ This small (30 rooms), charming hotel is in a quiet neighbourhood, but is near a market, restaurants and cafés. Some rooms have balconies. ❸ 16 rue de Constantinople, 8th ❶ 01 45 22 21 64 Ⓦ www.hotel-paris-orient.com Ⓝ Metro: Europe, Villiers or St-Lazare

Hôtel Duminy Vendôme ££ Just a few blocks from the Louvre and the Jardin des Tuileries, this comfortable hotel is classic, yet modern, with coffee maker and Wi-Fi in the rooms. ❸ 3–5 rue du Mont Thabor, 1st ❶ 01 42 60 32 80 Ⓦ www.HotelDuminyVendome.com Ⓝ Metro: Tuileries, Concorde or Madeleine

Hôtel La Sanguine ££ The Sanguine has a convenient location (near the place de la Madeleine), friendly staff and good breakfasts for around €7. ❸ 6 rue de Surène, 8th ❶ 01 42 65 71 61 Ⓦ www.hotelsanguine@free.fr Ⓝ Metro: Madeleine

Villa Escudier ££ This charming villa, with its trees and garden is far from the city hubbub. ❸ 64 rue Escudier, 9th ❶ 01 48 25 55 33 Ⓦ www.villaescudier.com Ⓝ Metro: Boulogne Jean Jaurès

Hôtel Atala £££ The 48-room Atala near the Champs-Élysées has a bright, cheery garden for fair-weather breakfasting and dining. The hotel is roomy by Parisian standards, and the upper floors

have good views. ⓐ 10 rue Chateaubriand, 8th ⓣ 01 45 62 01 62
ⓦ www.hotel-atala.com ⓝ Metro: Charles de Gaulle-Etoile

RIGHT BANK EAST

Caron de Beaumarchais £ Beautifully decorated (perhaps over-elaborate for some tastes), friendly and well located. ⓐ 12 rue Vieille du Temple, 4th ⓣ 01 42 72 34 12 ⓦ www.carondebeaumarchais.com ⓝ Metro: Hôtel de Ville

Hôtel du 7ème Art £ This unusual little hotel has a Hollywood theme, with numerous posters, photos and other memorabilia from the golden

⬥ *The charming Caron de Beaumarchais hotel*

era of movies. Rooms are small, and there is no lift. ⓐ 20 rue Saint-Paul, 4th
ⓣ 01 44 54 85 00 ⓦ www.paris-hotel-7art.com ⓝ Metro: St-Paul

Hôtel Saint Merry £ This unique hotel in the heart of the historical
Marais quarter, originally a presbytery, then a brothel, is in a restored
18th-century stone building with lots of character. ⓐ 78 rue de
la Verrerie, 4th ⓣ 01 42 78 14 15 ⓦ www.hotel-saintmerry.com
ⓝ Metro: St-Paul

Hôtel de Lutèce ££ Set in a 17th-century building, this has
a pleasant lobby, a fireplace, and huge, wooden beams across
the high, white-washed ceiling. The 23 small rooms are tastefully
decorated. ⓐ 65 rue Saint-Louis-en-l'Île, 4th ⓣ 01 43 26 23 52
ⓦ www.paris-hotel-lutece.com ⓝ Metro: Pont Marie

LEFT BANK

Hôtel Cluny Sorbonne £ Set in an 18th-century building in the
centre of the Latin Quarter, the hotel is within walking distance
of attractions such as Notre-Dame, the Panthéon and the Louvre.
Rimbaud, the great French poet, stayed here in 1872. ⓐ 8 rue Victor
Cousin, 5th ⓣ 01 43 54 66 66 ⓕ 01 43 29 68 07 ⓦ www.hotel-cluny.fr
ⓝ Metro: Cluny-La Sorbonne

Hôtel des Marronniers ££ A private courtyard entrance leads to this
charming hotel, whose garden is a haven in the centre of the city.
ⓐ 21 rue Jacob, 6th ⓣ 01 43 25 30 60 ⓦ www.hotel-marronniers.com
ⓝ Metro: Odéon or Saint-Germain-des-Prés

Hôtel du Panthéon ££ A cosy, Louis XVI-style hotel conveniently located
near rue Mouffetard, with a view of both the Panthéon and Sacré-Coeur.

ⓐ 19 pl. du Panthéon, 5th ⓣ 01 43 54 32 95 ⓦ www.hoteldupantheon.com
ⓝ Metro Cardinal Lemoine or Cluny-La Sorbonne

Hôtel de Buci £££ Near fashionable boulevard Saint-Germain,
the Buci is soothingly atmospheric, with leather chairs in the lobby,
potted palms and an intriguing collection of art deco paintings.
ⓐ 22 rue Buci, 6th ⓣ 01 55 42 74 74 ⓦ www.bucihotel.com
ⓝ Metro: Saint-Germain-des-Prés or Mabillon

HOSTELS

A network of youth hostels (*Auberges de Jeunesse*) offers comfortable,
inexpensive accommodation for members. There are also numerous
youth accommodation centres that don't require membership. The
website ⓦ www.parisinfo.com lists hostels, campsites and long-stay
apartments. The following are good choices:

Auberge Internationale des Jeunes £ The age limit here is 27 years
old. There are 160 beds, with rooms priced at €14 per person per
night from March to October, €13 from November to February.
Breakfast and bed linen are included. ⓐ 10 rue Trousseau, 11th
ⓣ 01 47 00 62 00 ⓦ www.aijparis.com ⓝ Metro: Ledru Rollin

3 Ducks Hostel £ Dormitories for four to eight persons. Prices from
€19 to €23 per person per night in winter (€23 to €26 in summer).
ⓐ 6 pl. Etienne Pernet, 15th ⓣ 01 48 42 04 05 ⓦ www.3ducks.fr
ⓝ Metro: Commerce

CAMPSITE
Camping du Bois de Boulogne £ This is the only campsite within Paris.
ⓐ 2 allée du Bord de l'Eau, 16th ⓣ 01 45 24 30 00 ⓦ www.campingparis.fr

THE BEST OF PARIS

TOP 10 ATTRACTIONS

- **Tour Eiffel (Effiel Tower)** The graceful, filigreed metal tower, glowing burnished gold at night, is the symbol of France around the world (see page 106)

- **Arc de Triomphe** Built to honour Napoleon's victories, this grand, angular arch stands in the centre of 12 avenues, the most famous of which is the Champs-Élysées (see page 62)

- **Notre-Dame** Like a silent sentinel, this magnificent Gothic cathedral on an island in the Seine has witnessed some of France's greatest events (see pages 84–5)

- **Seine** This aquatic artery meandering for 13 km (7 1/2 miles) through Paris is the exquisite heart of the city (see page 105)

- **Montmartre** Many visitors may know Montmartre through the movies, since this, and the adjacent Pigalle, is the famed historic, artistic area of the Moulin Rouge and the picturesque, magical world of Amélie Poulain (see pages 67–8)

- **Musée du Louvre** Once home of the kings of France, the 800-year-old Louvre could be called the king of museums, renowned the world over and housing works from ancient civilisations, the mid-1900s, and everything in between (see pages 68–9)

- **Cimetière du Père-Lachaise** Probably the world's most famous cemetery, Père-Lachaise is the final, beautiful resting place of some of France's most illustrious figures from Balzac to Piaf (see page 83)

- **Quartier Latin (Latin Quarter)** This lively area is the heart of the Left Bank. Once famous for its students and literary legacy, it is now buzzing with cafés and bistros, nightclubs and chic boutiques (see pages 103–5)

- **Musée d'Orsay** The former 19th-century train station is now renowned for its collection of Western art from 1848 to 1914 (see pages 109–11)

- **Markets** Integral to the daily life of Paris are its markets, from abundant fresh food markets to speciality markets selling anything from birds to bric-à-brac (see page 102)

Notre-Dame cathedral stands right in the centre of Paris

Suggested itineraries

HALF-DAY: PARIS IN A HURRY

If you have only half a day in Paris, taking the Batobus (see page 105) the length of the Seine from the Notre-Dame (see pages 84–5) to the

⬥ *Notre-Dame is beautiful from any angle*

Eiffel Tower (see page 106) or vice versa and visiting each monument at either end will give a compact, visually stunning introduction to Paris.

1 DAY: TIME TO SEE A LITTLE MORE

As well as the Batobus or an hour-long tour on one of the many sightseeing boats, such as the Bateaux Parisiens (see page 105), you should fit in a half-day tour of either the Musée du Louvre (see page 68) or the Musée d'Orsay (see page 109).

2–3 DAYS: TIME TO SEE MUCH MORE

Adding to one of the above itineraries, climb to the top of the Arc de Triomphe (see page 62) for a real perspective of the grand design of Paris, especially the broad boulevards stretching out like a star. A stroll down the Champs-Élysées, with its elegant shops and cafés, is a must. Over on the Left Bank, do as the Parisians do, visit a gallery or museum, then have a coffee at one of the famous literary cafés (see pages 113–14), watching the *beau monde* go by and soaking up the ambience of the Latin Quarter.

LONGER: ENJOYING PARIS TO THE FULL

Explore the *butte* (or hill) of Paris at Montmartre, where the Place du Tertre behind the white-domed Sacré-Coeur is the quintessential Parisian painters' corner. Licensed painters sell portraits or depictions of your favourite Parisian scene. From in front of the Sacré-Coeur, the rooftops of Paris stretch out below. Montmartre, with its climbing cobbled streets, is a great area to have a coffee or a meal.

If you have time to explore beyond Paris, you may wish to visit Versailles, the grand château and gardens built for Louis XIV, particularly if you can time your visit for the Grandes Eaux Musicales (see page 9) or the Nocturnes (see page 10).

Something for nothing

In Paris many wonderful experiences are there for the taking. The national museums, for example, are free on the first Sunday of every month. These include the Louvre, the Musée d'Orsay, the Conciergerie, the Panthéon, the Musée National du Moyen Age (in the Thermes gallo-romains and the Hôtel de Cluny), the Musée Rodin, the Musée Picasso and the Musée National des Arts Asiatiques-Guimet. Every Wednesday night the Maison Européenne de la Photographie has free entrance.

The permanent collections of all Paris City Council museums are also free. One of these, the **Musée Carnavalet**, displays the history of Paris from the French Revolution to today (🅐 23 rue de la Sevigne, 3rd ❶ 01 44 59 58 58 Ⓦ www.carnavalet.paris.fr). If you are interested in fashion, the **Palais Galliera** displays three centuries of history gratis, but check before you go as the fragility of the costumes does not allow the museum to be opened to the public year-round (🅐 10 av. Pierre 1er de Serbie, 16th ❶ 01 56 52 86 20 Ⓦ www.galliera.paris.fr).

Also in the Marais district is the 17th-century Place des Vosges. Ruddy-pink brick pavilions form a handsome square that is both a peaceful public space and a collection of art galleries. Nobility and literary figures, such as Victor Hugo, lived here and his house is now a museum.

Nearby, the fence along the famous Jardin du Luxembourg has become an outdoor photo gallery. Huge photographs, many by news photographers and photojournalists, are exhibited. Each is lit at night, providing an enchanting nocturnal experience.

During Paris's long, sultry summers, free concerts are held in some 20 parks and gardens and there is often a Latin or African drumbeat to be heard along the quays of central Paris.

The city itself is a walkable feast, and perhaps nowhere can you get more value for your nothing spent than strolling along the Seine. Each side of the river, from the Notre-Dame curving westward to the Eiffel Tower, provides a panorama of some of the world's most famous buildings and of the bridges that link Left Bank to Right.

⬤ *Under the Louvre's Pyramid – free entry on the first Sunday of each month*

When it rains

Rainy days are no problem in Paris, filled as it is with so many wonderful museums. Most are open through the weekend (closing on either Monday or Tuesday), and many, such as the Louvre, the Musée d'Orsay and the Maillol, have charming cafés to lounge in.

A particularly atmospheric retreat is the 5th-floor Rivoli restaurant in the BHV department store near the Hôtel de Ville. The Rivoli's star attraction is the panoramic view of the Paris rooftops, particularly the Hôtel de Ville, the Panthéon and many old buildings with their mansard roofs and chimneypots. Parisian cafés and brasseries in general are an integral part of the soul of the city. Simple, traditional establishments or fancier venues with polished brass and wood fittings are wonderful places to escape the rain, relax and watch life go by.

One way to get an instant briefing on Paris on a rainy day is to catch a screening of the excellent film *Paris Story*. In this multimedia promenade through Paris's past, 2,000 years of history plays out on a giant screen, with the character of Victor Hugo narrating.

Even for non-shoppers, the glass-covered passages of Paris are a delightful legacy of the early 19th century. Originally constructed to protect shoppers from wet weather, they still do so today, while housing luxury goods and boutiques. Among the most charming of the remaining arcades are the Grand-Cerf at 145 rue Saint-Denis, with its designer boutiques, and the *galeries* Colbert and Vivienne, at 16 rue des Petits-Champs, known for book collections and haute couture. All three are in the 2nd *arrondissement*.

Paris Story ⓐ 11 bis rue Scribe, 9th ❶ 01 42 66 62 06
Ⓦ www.exploreparis.fr ❺ shows on the hour 10.00–18.00
Ⓦ Metro: Opéra

◗ *Try the Rivoli restaurant in the BHV department store*

On arrival

TIME DIFFERENCE

Paris is on European standard time (GMT plus one hour). Daylight saving applies, with clocks going forward one hour in spring and back one hour in autumn, on the same date as the UK.

ARRIVING

By air

Paris has two main airports, Roissy-Charles de Gaulle (CDG) north of the city, and Orly. The easiest way to the city centre from both is by RER B commuter train. The line goes to Gare du Nord, Châtelet (centre of the Right Bank), Saint-Michel and Luxembourg (Left Bank). There are metro connections from those stations.

Those not travelling light can take Air France buses, which leave every 15 minutes for Porte Maillot and Charles de Gaulle-Etoile (Arc de Triomphe), or to the train stations of Gare de Lyon and Gare Montparnasse. There is also a service from Orly to Montparnasse and Invalides (for information in English ☎ 0892 350 820 and see ⓦ www.cars-airfrance.com). The RATP also operates cheap bus services: the Roissybus to rue Scribe (behind Opéra) and the Orlybus to Denfert-Rochereau (see ⓦ www.ratp.fr).

The most comfortable way to get to the city is by taxi. From the CDG airport to the centre of Paris will cost about €50 to €60, but could be higher during rush hours and traffic jams. There is a surcharge after 19.00 on Sundays and public holidays. Many drivers don't speak much English, so have your destination address written out. Taxis from Orly will be about €35 to €60 with normal traffic conditions. Drivers usually charge a fee for bags. Avoid touts inside the airport offering taxi or limousine service, as you will invariably end up paying much more. Go to the taxi ranks outside the terminal instead.

Several companies provide a minivan service, with delivery to hotels, but you have to book in advance, and you may have to share with other passengers (see 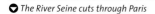 www.parisinfo.com).

Some charter airlines, and Ryanair, use Beauvais Airport, which is quite far from the city. Buses leave from the airport car park for the city shortly after each landing. You can also use a combination of taxi and train to get to Gare du Nord. For return flights, buses leave from Hôtel Concorde Lafayette on boulevard Pershing. You need to get to the hotel three-and-a-quarter hours before your flight departure time.
Beauvais ⓦ www.aeroportbeauvais.com
Roissy-Charles de Gaulle and Orly ⓦ www.adp.fr

⬤ *The River Seine cuts through Paris*

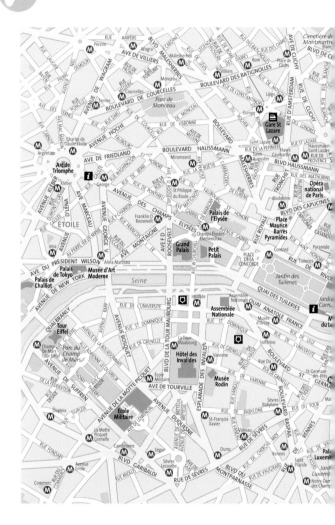

Paris

By rail

Those travelling on Eurostar from Britain arrive at Gare du Nord, which is on the metro. From here, RER B goes into the city (central stations are Châtelet and Saint-Michel). Alternatively, there is a taxi stand at the right-hand side of the station after disembarking the Eurostar.

By road

Driving into, or around, Paris is not for the faint-hearted. Traffic is heavy and hectic, parking spaces are hard to find and the one-way systems can be complex. If you still wish to drive, the main roads into Paris all reach the *périphérique* (ring road), which has various

IF YOU GET LOST, TRY …

Excuse me, do you speak English?
Excusez-moi, vous parlez anglais?
Ekskeweh mwah, voopahrlay ahnglay?

Excuse me, is this the right way to the old town/the city centre/the tourist office/the station/the bus station?
Excusez-moi, c'est la bonne direction pour la vieille ville/ le centre-ville/l'office de tourisme/la gare/la gare routière?
Ekskewzaymwah, seh lah bon deerekseeawng poor lah veeay veel/ ler sahngtr veel/lohfeece de tooreezm/lah gahr/lah gahr rootyair?

Can you point to it on my map?
Pouvez-vous me le montrer sur la carte?
Poovehvoo mer ler mawngtreh sewr lah kart?

exits to different parts of the city. Those arriving from the UK by car will probably use the A1 from the north.

Despite competition from the Chunnel, ferry and hydrofoil services continue to take cars and foot passengers across the English Channel.

FINDING YOUR FEET

Tourist office welcome centres at Gare du Nord, Pyramides, Louvre, Opéra, Gare de Lyon, Anvers (Montmartre), Porte de Versailles, Clemenceau (Champs-Élysées) provide free maps in ten languages. The telephone answering service is available 24 hours a day on ☏ 08 92 68 30 00

Nearly all hotels provide good complimentary maps featuring streets as well as the metro system. Be sure to get the hotel's *carte de visite* (business card) and keep it with you in case you get lost.

Violent crime is generally rare, but areas around train and bus stations, particularly Gare du Nord, have an increasing reputation for violence at night. There are many pickpockets in Paris, especially on the metro during rush hours and at crowded tourist attractions. Leave valuables in the hotel or room safe. Always be vigilant and keep bags and wallets closed and out of reach. Don't be obvious: carrying big bulky cameras and purses will attract pickpockets.

Always go to an official sales point to buy tickets, and avoid touts. If you encounter any problems, look for a uniformed police officer, transport security staff or ticket sales staff.

ORIENTATION

Paris is divided into 20 *arrondissements* (districts). The 1st is the centre of the city, and the others are laid out in a clockwise spiral from there. As the *arrondissements* are so basic to the layout of Paris, they are constantly referred to in guides and literature, almost always using

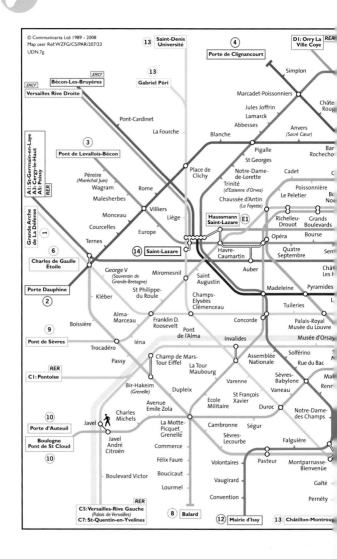

© Communicarta Ltd 1989 - 2008
Map user Ref: WZFG/CS/PAR/207/23
UDN.7g

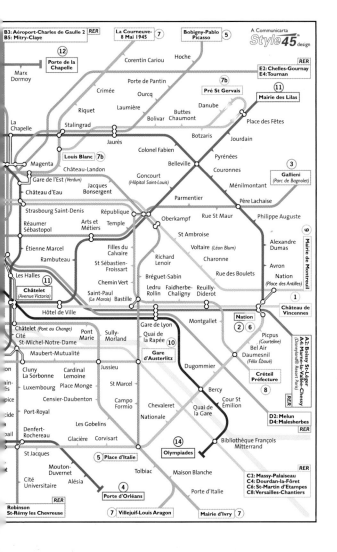

simply their associated number (1st, 2nd, etc, as in the addresses in this guide). The Seine divides the city into Left and Right Banks.

The best way to get to know Paris is to walk around the hotel neighbourhood. Paris is like a series of villages, each with its own attraction and character. Then you can begin to explore further afield by public transport. The main city thoroughfares include the Champs-Élysées and boulevard Haussmann on the Right Bank, and boulevards Saint-Germain and Saint-Michel on the Left.

Paris is a small city, easy to navigate on foot. You can walk across it from east to west or north to south in one day, if you don't stop for sightseeing. However, it is not always pedestrian-friendly, so it is important to be alert, especially at crossings.

If you get lost, some metro stops have maps displaying the immediate area. You can also get your bearings from the Eiffel Tower, Arc de Triomphe, Panthéon, Notre-Dame or Tour Montparnasse.

GETTING AROUND

Paris has an excellent metro system reaching all parts of the city. The 14 lines are identified by number and colour. The RER commuter trains connect to the suburbs. An RATP 'Paris Visite' is a travel pass for one, two, three or five consecutive days on metro, bus and RER trains, NOT including trips to the airport. A one-day adult pass for one to three zones is €8.50; a five-day pass for the same zones is €27.20. A single €1.40 metro ticket can be used for one journey by metro, train or bus in zones one and two, including all connections. Tickets can be purchased singly or in a *carnet* (book) of ten for €10.50 at the ticket offices or machines in metro stations, and also in some tobacconists. Keep your ticket until you have completed your journey; on the RER and some metro stations you will need it to exit the system. Note that the entire Paris metro network is a no-smoking zone.

Route maps for buses are available free in metro stations, and you can hail taxis in the street or at taxi ranks. Paris has recently introduced a hop-on, hop-off bike system called *Vélib*. There are 750 stations spread around the city where you may collect or deposit a bike. All you need to do is subscribe for a day, a week or a year and you're away. Check ☎ 01 30 79 79 30 or Ⓦ www.velib.paris.fr for details.

◗ *Even the underground stations are pretty*

PARIS IN THE MOVIES

If, on a first trip to Paris, you find that various parts of the city are weirdly familiar, it doesn't necessarily mean that the reincarnationists are right: the city has formed the backdrop to so many popular films over the years that you could easily have absorbed its picturesque settings simply by spending rainy afternoons curled up in front of the telly.

Paris is all over the movies, and this is apt when you consider that commercial cinema was born here, when Louis and Auguste Lumière projected their first films in the basement of the Grand Café on the boulevard des Capucines in 1895. Since then, more than 400 major motion pictures have been shot among Paris's tree-lined boulevards and broad quays.

Many have depicted the clichéd Paris of accordion music, the cancan and the wise-cracking prostitute with a heart of gold; and the city lends itself to the visual commonplace, too. Countless films use establishing shots of Gustave Eiffel's imposing wrought-iron tower, and another popular backdrop, the Seine, is also over-familiar to movie fans.

Robert Altman's 1994 *Prêt-à-Porter* may have been a box-office flop, but at least it managed to juxtapose unglamorous images of the city's traffic jams, rain and grey skies with an idyllic, tourist-video vision of its scenery. As the city changes, films become unwitting historical documents: take, for example, the 1963 comedy *Irma la Douce* (featuring the saintly hooker figure); this has preserved excellent images of the giant food markets of Les Halles, which moved out of central Paris in 1969.

Paris is fabulous if you want to explore themes that are in any way to do with sex. Its seamier aspects are perfect for portraying windswept-and-interesting desires, hence Brando's pursuit of Maria Schneider along the Bir-Hakeim Bridge in Bernardo Bertolucci's darkly erotic *Last Tango in Paris* (1972). In fact, Paris's sometimes-brooding majesty often manages to disguise the essential ludicrousness of such films.

Numerous movies are set in the clubs of racy, *fin-de-siècle* Paris and gain atmosphere from the city's reputation for sauciness. The 1952 *Moulin Rouge*, with José Ferrer as diminutive poster boy Toulouse-Lautrec, evokes Paris's raunchy belle époque nightlife so vividly that it's planted images of absinthe, smoky cabarets, raffish sociopaths and slinky *chanteuses* in many impressionable minds. As unrealistic as it was, it conveyed more truth than the computer-generated, too-comfortable Paris of 2001's *Moulin Rouge*.

Amélie, the big French hit of 2001, takes place in a *moulin* of a different sort, just a few minutes' walk from the infamous club. The film's elfin heroine devises her altruistic schemes at the Café Tabac des Deux Moulins on 15 rue Lepic, which is now on many a cinephile's must-see list. The bar and the rest of this lively *quartier* are clearly recognisable all through the film. One awaits a sequel, in which impish Amélie's purity of soul will have led her to the inevitable career change, as we see her walking Paris's cinematic streets in fishnets and a red beret, transforming the lives of her diminutive-but-raffish punters by curing their addiction to absinthe with a blast on her accordion. Cliché, of course, but the urban scenery will be fantastic.

SNCF trains to out-of-town areas depart from these *gares* (stations): Gare du Nord, Gare de l'Est, St Lazare, Lyon, Austerlitz and Montparnasse.

RATP provides information in English on buses, metro and RER commuter trains ☎ 08 92 68 41 14 ⓦ www.ratp.com

SNCF ☎ 01 53 90 20 20 ⓦ www.transilien.com

CAR HIRE

It is not a good idea to rent a car to use in Paris or to get to out-of-town places. For travelling around Île-de-France or throughout the country, it is better to take the excellent, efficient SNCF trains and hire a car at your destination. For information, see ⓦ www.voyages-sncf.com

If you do wish to hire a car in Paris, you will find all the major car-rental companies here, all with offices at Charles de Gaulle airport. Rates range from about €30 a day up to more than €100.

Avis ☎ 0820 05 05 05 ⓦ www.avis.com

Europcar ☎ 0825 358 358 ⓦ www.europcar.com

Hertz ☎ 0825 861 861 ⓦ www.hertz.com

National ☎ 01 53 20 06 52 ⓦ www.nationalcar.com

Thrifty ☎ 01 43 47 58 80 ⓦ www.thrifty.com

▶ *Paris has a variety of architectural styles*

Right Bank West

The traditional separation of Paris into Left and Right Bank, between business and culture, is no longer valid. The Left Bank still has most of the universities (especially the Sorbonne) and the bohemian cafés, but today the Right Bank also has artistic areas, especially the Marais and the Bastille. Both sides of the Seine have their distinct charm and attractions. For ease of sightseeing, we have divided the city into three areas: Right Bank West, Right Bank East and Left Bank.

Under the direction of Napoleon III, Baron Georges Haussmann reshaped and modernised Paris. His work is most obvious in this area of the city, with its broad, tree-lined boulevards, magnificent monuments, grand mansions and open gardens. Some of the city's greatest sights are found here, such as the Louvre, the Champs-Élysées and Arc de Triomphe, Montmartre and Sacré-Coeur.

SIGHTS & ATTRACTIONS

Arc de Triomphe

Built to honour Napoleon's victories, this grand arch is the centrepiece of 12 boulevards that radiate 360 degrees from it. Stairs lead 50 m (164 ft) up to its roof for a panoramic view of the symmetry of Paris. La Voie Royale runs from the Louvre to the modern Grande Arche in the Place de la Défense. Beneath the Arc de Triomphe, a flame burns for an unknown soldier from World War I. There's free admission on the first Sunday of the month during winter. ⓐ pl. du Général-de-Gaulle, 8th ❶ 01 55 37 73 77 ⓦ www.monum.fr ❶ 10.00–23.00 (summer); 10.00–22.30 (winter) ⓝ Metro/RER A: Charles de Gaulle Etoile ❶ closed on all major public holidays

Paris Right Bank West

Champs-Élysées

This is the grandest of the boulevards that stretch away from the Arc de Triomphe. Luxury boutiques and car showrooms, nightclubs and the *beau monde* are all here. Having a coffee on 'the Champs' isn't cheap, but the passing parade is worth the price. At night, with the Arc floodlit in golden light, the Champs is certainly impressive. However, despite the boulevard's grand demeanour, not all prices are grand. You can have a lot of good, clean fun on the Champs.

Metro: Charles de Gaulle Etoile

Conciergerie

One of the oldest buildings in Paris, the conical-towered Conciergerie on the Île de la Cité, once a palace, became a prison during the French Revolution. Among the 2,800 prisoners held here, the most famous was Marie-Antoinette, who was taken to the guillotine at Place de la Concorde. Her cell can be seen today. Guided visits are available.

2 blvd du Palais, 1st 01 53 40 60 80 www.monum.fr 09.30–18.00 (summer); 09.00–17.00 (winter) Metro: Cité

Jardin des Tuileries

The Tuileries, Paris's oldest park, forms an orderly sweep of greenery, gardens and statues leading up to the Louvre, affording wonderful views of the museum buildings in one direction and the Arc de Triomphe in the other. The park is also a sculpture garden, with works by Rodin, Henry Moore and Max Ernst, among others. A recent addition, loved and targeted in equal measure by birds, is Giuseppe Penone's *Arbre des Voyelles (The Vowel Tree)*, a bronze fallen tree. At its western end, the park is graced by the exposition spaces **Galerie Nationale du Jeu de Paume** (www.jeudepaume.org) displaying photography and contemporary art exhibitions, and the **Musée de l'Orangerie**

⬤ *Old and new sculptural forms to enjoy in the Jardin des Tuileries*

◆ The cupolas of the majestic basilica of Sacré-Coeur bask in the evening sun

(w www.musee-orangerie.fr), with paintings by Monet, Renoir, Modigliani and Picasso among others. a rue de Rivoli, 1st ● 07.30–21.00 (summer); 07.30–19.30 (winter) ● Metro: Tuileries or Concorde

Montmartre

This historic district in the 18th *arrondissement*, called the 'balcony of Paris', is characterised by Sacré-Coeur, steep streets lined with ancient buildings, and a lively buzz from the tourists and locals congregating at terrace cafés, restaurants, crowded boutiques and around the basilica. This is the area immortalised by Toulouse-Lautrec in his paintings and posters of the Moulin Rouge (still extant and still saucy) and thrilling cancan girls. Nearby Pigalle advertises in loud neon its sex shows and wares. Like a cartoon locomotive, the little white Montmartrain tootles through the cobbled streets, giving commentary in several languages. It departs in front of the Sacré-Coeur or the Place Pigalle (● 01 48 00 90 80).

Crowning Montmartre with white cupolas, the basilica of **Sacré-Coeur** is one of the most visible of Paris's landmarks. It is especially beautiful on bright, blue days or glowing pearl-white at night, but the stone is loveliest when glistened with rain. Those with the energy can climb up the main rotunda. At weekends, especially in summer, the steps and grounds of the basilica are crowded with sightseers, entertained by an assortment of performers and buskers.

The **Place du Tertre** is an ancient square just west of the Sacré-Coeur and is the quintessential artist-with-easel scene. Its picture-postcard ambience has made it crowded, though, so you may have to take a rest in one of the neighbourhood cafés or wine bars. There is even a Montmartre wine, and a tiny vineyard nearby (between rue des Saules and rue Saint-Vincent).

PARIS MUSEUM PASS

If one of your reasons for coming to Paris is to make
a lot of museum visits, the Paris Museum Pass will save
you time and money. The Pass allows you to jump queues
and gives unlimited access to over 60 museums and
monuments. You can buy cards for two, four or six days.
See Ⓦ www.parismuseumpass.com for prices and details.

If you're hanging out for some retail therapy, boutiques in
the **Place des Abbesses**, west of the Sacré-Coeur, have a relaxed
atmosphere on Sundays, when most Paris shops are closed.
Sacré-Coeur ⓐ 35 rue du Chevalier-de-la-Barre, 18th ① 01 53 41 89 00
🄱 Basilica 06.00–22.30, Dome and crypt 09.30–18.30 Ⓜ Metro:
Anvers or Abbesses

Musée du Louvre

One of the world's largest museums, the Musée du Louvre exhibits
only 10 per cent of its works. It is renowned for such masterpieces
as the *Mona Lisa* (affectionately called *La Joconde* by the French),
the *Venus de Milo, Winged Victory, Psyche and Cupid,* Da Vinci's *Virgin
and Child with St Anne* and Géricault's *Raft of the Medusa.* With some
eight departments and 35,000 works on display, the Louvre could be
daunting to those trying to take in its immensity of riches. Yet rooms
with polished wood floors and warm lighting are immediately inviting.
The best approach is to pick a favourite period and hone in on that.
You won't see it all, so relax and enjoy. The wonders that you do see
will provide a lifetime of memories.

Even if you're not visiting the Louvre, you can walk through Passage Richelieu off the rue de Rivoli to view some of the museum's wondrous marble and bronze sculptures through large windows. Upon entering the central courtyard, the Cour Napoléon, you'll see I M Pei's *Pyramid* of glass and rivets. This modern structure, which is the museum's main entrance, has provoked considerable controversy, with many complaining that it spoiled the symmetry of the old buildings. Yet with the ancient structures reflected in the modern one and fountains further softening the transition, most visitors feel that the effect is a harmonious juxtaposition of palace and pyramid.

ⓐ rue de Rivoli, 1st ① 01 40 20 50 50 ⓛ 09.00–18.00 (until 21.45 Wed & Fri), closed Tues Ⓝ Metro: Palais Royal Musée du Louvre

⬤ *Even exterior views of the Louvre are works of art*

Place de la Concorde

The golden-tipped obelisk in the centre is actually a 3,200-year-old
Egyptian relic from Luxor. This bright grand square has a bloody
history: during the French Revolution, more than 1,000 people were
guillotined here, including King Louis XVI and Marie-Antoinette.
Ⓜ Metro: Concorde

Sainte-Chapelle

This delicate gem among Paris churches is renowned for its 13th-
century stained-glass windows, whose 15-m (49-ft) compositions fill
the chapel with jewels of light. ⓐ 4 blvd du Palais, 1st ☎ 01 53 40 60 80
Ⓦ www.monum.fr 🕐 09.30–18.00 (summer); 09.00–17.00 (winter)
Ⓜ Metro: Cité

Tenniseum

The Stade Roland-Garros, where the French Open is held, is open
for visits when there are no matches. The first multimedia tennis
museum, the Tenniseum, covers some 2,200 sq m (23,681 sq ft).
There are also guided tours of the museum and stadium.
ⓐ 2 av. Gordon-Bennett, 16th ☎ 01 47 43 48 48 Ⓦ www.fft.fr
or www.rolandgarros.com 🕐 10.00–18.00, closed Mon
Ⓜ Metro: Porte d'Auteuil

Trocadéro

A half-moon shaped structure on the Right Bank facing the Eiffel
Tower, the Palais de Chaillot (called the Trocadéro), was built for
the 1937 Exposition Universelle. It houses the Musée de l'Homme
(☎ 01 44 05 72 72 Ⓦ www.mnhn.fr), the Musée National de
la Marine (☎ 01 53 65 69 69 Ⓦ www.musee-marine.fr 🕐 closed
Tues) and the Théâtre National de Chaillot (☎ 01 53 65 30 00

Ⓦ www.theatre-chaillot.fr). The Cité de l'Architecture et du Patrimoine finally completely opened here in September 2007 (Ⓦ www.citechaillot.fr Ⓣ 01 58 51 52 00). In summer, people chill out around the Trocadéro's cool pools and lawns. The central square, where the wings of the building cleave in two, reveals a magnificent view of the Eiffel Tower. Ⓐ 17 pl. du Trocadéro, 16th Ⓜ Metro: Trocadéro

CULTURE

Galeries Nationales du Grand Palais

With its splendid belle époque glass roof visible along the Seine's Right Bank, this grand palace built for the 1900 World Fair holds major art exhibitions. Ⓐ 3 av. du General Eisenhower, 8th Ⓣ 01 44 13 17 17 Ⓦ www.rmn.fr Ⓛ 10.00–20.00, until 22.00 Wed & Fri, closed Tues Ⓜ Metro: Champs-Élysées Clemenceau or Franklin-Roosevelt

Musée d'Art Moderne de la Ville de Paris

The city's modern art museum champions artists such as Steve McQueen. Next door, the Palais de Tokyo (Ⓣ 01 47 23 38 86 Ⓛ 12.00–midnight, closed Mon) is a grand display case for contemporary art. Ⓐ 11 av. du Président Wilson, 16th Ⓣ 01 53 67 40 00 Ⓦ www.paris.fr/musees Ⓛ 10.00–18.00 (until 20.00 Wed for temporary exhibitions), closed Mon Ⓜ Metro: Iéna

Musée Dapper

This small, intimate space displays African art, from sub-Sahara to the diasporas of the continent. Ⓐ 35 rue Paul Valéry, 16th Ⓣ 01 45 00 91 75 Ⓦ www.dapper.com.fr Ⓛ 11.00–19.00, closed Tues, free admission on the last Wed of the month Ⓜ Metro: Victor Hugo

Musée Marmottan Monet

This lovely museum, in what was once a private home, houses
a large collection of Impressionists, among other works, particularly
The Water Lilies and other masterpieces by Monet. 2 rue Louis-
Boilly, 16th 01 44 96 50 33 www.marmottan.com
 10.00–18.00, closed Mon Metro: La Muette

Musée National des Arts Asiatiques-Guimet

This is one of the world's best collections of Asian art. Some
45,000 objects include works from China, Japan, India and Southeast
Asia. Its annex, the **Panthéon Bouddhique** (19 av. d'Iena, 16th
 01 40 73 88 00 09.45–17.45 Wed–Thur), is a little-known jewel
with ancient Buddhist statues, a Japanese garden and tea pavilion.
The garden, a tiny oasis, has stands of bamboo, trickling waterfalls,
wooden walkways and flowers. 6 pl. d'Iena, 16th 01 56 52 53 00
 www.museeguimet.fr 10.00–18.00 Wed–Thur Metro: Iéna

Musée du Vieux Montmartre

This is a hidden treasure in a charming 17th-century building
entered through a small courtyard. The artists Duffy, Utrillo and
Renoir lived and worked here. 12 rue Cortot, 18th 01 49 25 89 37
 www.museedemontmartre.fr 11.00–18.00, closed Mon & Tues
 Metro: Lamarck-Caulaincourt or Abbesses

Palais Garnier: Opéra National de Paris

Built on the orders of Napoleon III, the Palais Garnier, with its
grand façade and foyer (both renovated in 2006), is a masterpiece
of 19th-century design. It was designed by Charles Garnier to
resemble a classical château. With its sweeping marble staircase,
mirrors and gilded mosaics in the grand foyer, sculptures and

painted ceiling depicting allegories of music, this awe-inspiring building is one of the most visited in Paris. The horseshoe-shaped auditorium has a ceiling painted by Marc Chagall. It offers a full programme of dance, ballet and opera year-round, except August. ⓐ pl. de l'Opéra, 2nd ⓣ 08 92 89 90 90, Guided tours 01 41 10 08 10 ⓦ www.operadeparis.fr ⓛ unaccompanied visits of the main areas 10.00–18.00, comprehensive 90-minute guided tours in English Wed, Sat & Sun (daily in July & Aug) ⓜ Metro: Opéra

Petit Palais

The city's sumptuous fine arts museum contains the spectrum of art from antiquities to early 20th century. There are also excellent temporary exhibitions. ⓐ av. Winston Churchill, 8th ⓣ 01 53 43 40 00 ⓦ www.petitpalais.paris.fr ⓛ 10.00–18.00 Tues–Sun, until 21.00 Tues for temporary shows ⓜ Metro: Champs-Élysées Clemenceau or Concorde

RETAIL THERAPY

The Golden Triangle of haute couture is here, extending from the Faubourg Saint-Honoré, the Place Vendôme and the rue Royale, to the rue Montaigne and the Champs-Élysées. Fashion boutiques in rue Etienne Marcel, in the 1st and 2nd *arrondissements*, have become recently hip with the showbiz set.

Carrousel du Louvre The inverted glass pyramid of the Louvre adds light and design drama to the Carrousel du Louvre. With its 45 boutiques and 14 restaurants, shoppers can keep occupied for hours. Goods range from fashion and jewellery to household items. Entrance on rue de Rivoli, through the museum or the metro.

ⓐ 99 rue de Rivoli, 1st ⓒ 08.30–23.00, Stores 07.00–20.00
ⓝ Metro: Palais Royal Musée du Louvre

🔺 *Galeries Lafayette with that special Christmas sparkle*

Colette Probably the hippest boutique in town, with accessories, bling, CDs, clothes, tech toys and trinkets for the seriously fashionable. There's a water bar downstairs with designer *eau* and a resident dog. ⓐ 213 rue Saint-Honoré, 1st ⓣ 01 55 35 33 90 ⓦ www.colette.fr ⓛ 11.00–19.00 Mon–Sat Ⓜ Metro: Tuileries or Pyramides

Cop Copine An original little *créateur boutique* for women that has clothes which are both comfortable and stylish. It can be a bit pricey, but you can get good discounts during the sales. There are two in Paris: ⓐ 80 rue Rambuteau (3rd) ⓣ 01 40 28 03 72 and ⓐ 37 rue Etienne Marcel (2nd) ⓣ 01 53 00 94 80.

Fauchon Taking up two corners of the Place de la Madeleine and with shops all over town, Fauchon is perhaps the most elegant gourmet food store in Paris, selling fine foods from chocolates and foie gras to teas since 1886. A mini rose-coloured bag with two chocolates will give friends back home a taste of Paris. ⓐ 26 pl. de la Madeleine, 6th ⓣ 01 70 39 38 00 ⓦ www.fauchon.com ⓛ 08.00–21.00, closed Sun Ⓜ Metro: Madeleine

Forum des Halles A sprawling subterranean shopping and cinema complex in the 1st *arrondissement*, this place buzzes with young shoppers, but the crowds can be crushing. ⓐ 101 Porte Berger ⓣ 01 44 76 96 56 ⓦ www.forumdeshalles.com ⓛ 10.00–19.30 Mon–Sat Ⓜ Metro: Châtelet

Galeries Lafayette In the Opéra district, this elegant Parisian department store has designer togs, an activewear department, a children's 'concept store', a separate building for men and a gourmet food section. The Lafayette Maison across the street (no. 35) has everything for the home. ⓐ 40 blvd Haussmann, 8th ☎ 01 42 82 34 56 ⓦ www.galerieslafayette.com ⓛ 09.30–19.30, until 21.00 Thur ⓝ Metro: Chaussée-d'Antin-Lafayette

Marché aux Puces de la Porte de Clignancourt You can find some gems tucked among the junk at this huge flea market, which extends beyond the *périphérique* (ring road) into Saint-Ouen. ⓐ av. de la Porte de Clignancourt, 8th ⓦ www.les-puces.com ⓛ 09.00–18.00 Sat–Mon ⓝ Metro: Porte de Clignancourt or Garibaldi

Le Printemps A department store near Galeries Lafayette that also stocks a wide variety of fashionable clothes and accessories. ⓐ 64 blvd Haussmann, 8th ☎ 01 42 82 50 00 ⓦ www.printemps.fr ⓛ 09.35–19.00, until 22.00 Thur ⓝ Metro: Havre-Caumartin

Zara With some 25 locations around Paris, this Spanish clothing store has copies of catwalk fashions at affordable prices. Items for men and children, too. ⓐ 2 rue Halévy, 9th ☎ 01 44 71 90 90 ⓛ 10.00–20.00 Mon–Sat ⓝ Metro: Opéra

TAKING A BREAK

Angelina £ ❶ This elegant patisserie and tea salon has a *fin-de-siècle* dining room as frothy as the pastries. Its hot chocolate is legendary. ⓐ 226 rue de Rivoli, 1st ☎ 01 42 60 82 00 ⓛ 08.00–19.00 Mon–Fri, 09.00–19.00 Sat & Sun ⓝ Metro: Tuileries

Cafés et Thés Verlet £ ❷ This cosy café features mirrors and old wood furnishings, canvas sacks of coffee beans and large old tea tins. You can purchase tea or coffee to take away or enjoy on the premises. ⓐ 256 rue Saint-Honoré, 1st ① 01 42 60 67 39 ⓛ 09.30–18.30 Mon–Sat Ⓜ Metro: Pyramides

Cojean £ ❸ Fast food's health food here and you can indulge in soups, sandwiches, salads and juices; plus, everything's fresh. ⓐ 4–6 rue de Sèze (off blvd de la Madeleine), 9th ① 01 40 06 08 80 Ⓦ www.cojean.fr ⓛ 10.00-18.00 Mon–Sat Ⓜ Metro: Madeleine

Ladurée £ ❹ This celebrated tea salon (established 1862) is known for its excellent pastries and ornate dining room. It's also famous for its melt-in-your-mouth macaroons. ⓐ 16 rue Royale, 8th ① 01 42 60 21 79 Ⓦ www.laduree.fr ⓛ 08.30–19.00 Mon–Sat, 10.00–19.00 Sun Ⓜ Metro: Madeleine

Au Progrès £ ❺ A simple café and bistro in Montmartre, with friendly staff and big picture windows from which to see the spires of the Sacré-Coeur peeking above the old buildings. ⓐ 7 rue des Trois Frères, 18th ① 01 42 64 07 37 ⓛ 09.00–02.00 Ⓜ Metro: Anvers

AFTER DARK

RESTAURANTS
Le Chartier £ ❻ Since 1896, this traditional French bistro has offered standard French fare in a crowded, high-ceilinged room. The lively, old-fashioned atmosphere is the main attraction. ⓐ 7 rue Faubourg Montmartre, 9th ① 01 47 70 86 29 ⓛ 11.30–15.00 & 18.00–22.00 Ⓜ Metro: Grands Boulevards ① tables cannot be booked, so you may have to queue

La Crypte de Polska £ 🔞 Ever dined in the crypt of a church?
This one, in the basement of a Polish church, sells such hearty
Polish fare as pork and cabbage dishes at reasonable prices.
🅐 1 pl. Maurice Barrès, 1st 🕔 01 42 60 43 33 🕔 12.00–15.00
& 19.00–22.00 Tues–Sun 🔵 Metro: Pyramides

Aux Vieux Châtelet £ 🔵 Simple French fare at reasonable prices
is offered by this traditional café-brasserie, which has a view of the
river and some of the city's oldest buildings. 🅐 1 pl. du Châtelet, 1st
🕔 01 42 33 79 27 🕔 07.00–23.30 🔵 Metro: Châtelet

Chez Cécile – La Ferme des Mathurins £–££ 🔵 Young chef Stéphane
Pitré works wonders with unusual ingredients here, and every
Thursday there's live jazz. 🅐 17 rue Vignon, 9th 🕔 01 42 66 46 39
🅦 www.chez-cecile.com 🕔 12.00–14.30 Mon–Fri, 19.00–22.30 Mon–Sat

Café Marly ££ 🔟 In the Louvre, this trendy café-restaurant serves
modern fare with a view of the sculptures and the glass pyramid.
🅐 93 rue de Rivoli, 1st 🕔 01 49 26 06 60 🕔 08.00–02.00
🔵 Metro: Palais Royal Musée du Louvre

La Fermette Marbeuf 1900 ££ 🔵 In this listed monument you
can dine in an art nouveau sun lounge and enjoy perfect service
and classic French cuisine. 🅐 5 rue Marbeuf, 8th 🕔 01 53 23 08 28
🅦 www.fermettemarbeuf.com 🕔 12.00–15.00, 19.00–23.30
🔵 Metro: Alma-Marceau or Franklin D Roosevelt

BARS, CLUBS & ENTERTAINMENT

Les Bains Douches This former bathhouse-turned-club has attained mythical status on the circuit. It features a newly opened restaurant, too. ⓐ 7 rue du Bourg-l'Abbé, 3rd ⓣ 01 48 87 01 80 ⓦ www.lesbainsdouches.net ⓛ 23.30–08.00 Tues–Sun ⓝ Metro: Etienne Marcel

Le Bar du Plaza Among the young French designers putting their distinctive stamp on Paris is Patrick Jouin, who has transformed the bar at the Hôtel Plaza Athénée into a hot nightspot with a cool idea: an 'iceberg' counter. The signature drink is the Rose Royale (champagne with raspberry purée). ⓐ 25 av. Montaigne, 8th ⓣ 01 53 67 66 65 ⓦ www.plaza-athenee-paris.com ⓛ 18.00–01.30 ⓝ Metro: Alma Marceau or Franklin D Roosevelt

Le Divan du Monde A great name ('the world's divan') for a great place that offers all styles of music and shows. ⓐ 75 rue des Martyrs, 9th ⓣ 01 40 05 06 99 ⓦ www.divandumonde.com ⓛ 20.00–02.00 ⓝ Metro: Pigalle

Le Duc des Lombards One of this music-loving city's best jazz clubs attracts aficionados with its big-name performers. ⓐ 42 rue des Lombards, 4th ⓣ 01 42 33 22 88 ⓛ 19.30–01.00 ⓝ Metro: Châtelet

Rex Club This popular club is great for hardcore dancers who like shaking to house, techno and electro. ⓐ 5 blvd Poissonnière, 2nd ⓣ 01 42 36 10 96 ⓦ www.rexclub.com ⓛ 23.30–06.00 ⓝ Metro: Bonne Nouvelle

Right Bank East

The Right Bank East is the oldest part of Paris, including Île de la Cité, Île Saint-Louis and the Marais. Much of it was untouched by the great modernisation of the 1860s, so here you still find ancient cobbled streets, small courtyards and medieval buildings that appear to sag and lean into the street. Its 10th, 19th and 20th *arrondissements* are called 'the people's Paris', while the Marais and the Bastille are hip; Bastille, particularly, hums with bars and clubs. The main attractions include the Notre-Dame cathedral, the Marais district, Canal St-Martin, the Bastille area with its modern opera house, and Père-Lachaise cemetery.

SIGHTS & ATTRACTIONS

Bastille

The column in the centre of the Place de la Bastille, topped by a golden liberty statue, is the symbol of the French Revolution. It was here, in 1789, that the people of Paris stormed the Bastille prison, freeing the prisoners and rising in arms against the excesses of the aristocrats and the royalty. The 51.5-m (nearly 170-ft) Colonne de Juillet commemorates the victims of two subsequent uprisings (in 1830 and 1848), who are buried in the crypt at its base. People still rally here today during major demonstrations. The metro station's brightly painted tiles depict scenes from the uprisings.

Today, the Bastille district in the 11th is a lively people place, with the modern Opéra Bastille and the streets surrounding the square providing a party atmosphere, especially at night and on weekends. Among the trendy clubs off the square is OPA (see After Dark, page 97). ⊕ Metro: Bastille

Canal Cruise

A different way to look at Paris is from a canal boat. The leisurely, two-and-a-half-hour cruise on the Canal St-Martin passes through numerous locks, under footbridges and along a 595-m (1/3 mile) vault of the Bastille, with the Japanese artist Keiichi Tahara's *Sounds of Light* laser light show dancing along the tunnel walls. The day-

🔺 *View from a canal*

long tour to the Marne River goes to the 'land of *guinguettes*' (riverside open-air dance clubs) and rural France. Canauxrama runs tours most days through the summer, but check with the company for a current schedule. Tours start from the Bastille's Port de l'Arsenal, a giant marina accommodating 200 boats, near the Bastille metro station. ⓐ Bassin de la Villette, 13 quai de la Loire, 19th ⓣ 01 42 39 15 00 ⓦ www.canauxrama.com ⓜ Metro: Bastille

Canal St-Martin

With pedestrian quays on both sides (Valmy and Jemmapes), Canal St-Martin is a pleasant waterway meandering from Paris-Arsenal port to La Villette basin. Little boutiques, bistros and cafés have made this promenade popular with walkers, cyclists, fishermen and rollerbladers. The Hôtel du Nord (ⓐ 102 quai de Jemmapes, 10th ⓣ 01 40 40 78 78), where the film of the same name was filmed, is now a pleasant, low-key restaurant that was voted Paris's trendiest venue by American *Elle* in 2006. ⓜ Metro: République

Cimetière du Père-Lachaise

Paris's first secular cemetery is now one of its most visited sights. Among the famous figures buried here are Molière, Apollinaire, Chopin, Modigliani, Proust and Oscar Wilde. Jim Morrison fans flock to his tomb in a never-ending pilgrimage. An elaborate, life-sized reclining bronze statue of playboy journalist Victor Noir, shot in a duel on 10 January, 1870, has become a fertility symbol, his prominent tumescence polished to a bright shine by generations of hopeful women. With its tree-lined alleys and flowers, the Père-Lachaise is like a garden, with 44 ha (109 acres) of greenery amid the tombs. The Mairie de Paris (ⓣ 01 43 28 27 63) conducts guided visits in English in July and August. ⓐ 16 rue du Repos, 20th ⓣ 01 55 25 82 10 ⓜ Metro: Père-Lachaise

Île Saint-Louis

Right behind Notre-Dame, Île Saint-Louis is actually made up
of two islets that joined together in 1614. Laundry women once
worked here, but now only the quayside façades remain, and rue
Saint-Louis-en-l'Île evokes that earlier era. Below, on hot summer
days, sunbathers stretch out and impromptu parties occur. On the
opposite banks, *bouquinistes* sell their second-hand books, postcards
and posters. Ⓝ Metro: Pont-Marie

Marais

One of the city's oldest areas, the Marais (a marsh drained to
make aristocrats' mansions in the 16th century) is an intimate area
of speciality boutiques, restaurants and museums. The district is
great for strolling, with its narrow streets, ancient timbered houses,
cobbled cloisters, fountains, squares, surprising architectural details
including a mosaic-covered building and houses so aged they lean
into the street. Many Marais shops, particularly on rue des
Francs-Bourgeois, are open on Sunday. Ⓝ Metro: St-Paul

Notre-Dame

With its dusky white towers rising above the Île de la Cité in the centre
of the Seine, the Notre-Dame cathedral, a Gothic masterpiece, is one
of the best-loved sights in Paris. Victor Hugo immortalised the cathedral
in his novel *Notre Dame de Paris*. The French version of the film of the
book (1957) has wonderful scenes of the hunchback and the gypsy
Esmeralda on the balcony of the towers, with jutting gargoyles and
views of Paris. Tower visits are free on the first Sunday of the month.

Often unnoticed, a brass plaque in the stones of the *parvis* (square)
in front of the Notre-Dame marks kilometre zero. Distances to various
destinations in France are marked from that point.

Directly in front of the cathedral, and overlooked by many sightseers, a staircase leads down to the archaeological Crypt of the Parvis of Notre-Dame (❸ 6 pl. du Parvis-de-Notre-Dame, Île de la Cité, 4th ❶ 01 55 42 50 10 Ⓦ www.cathedraledeparis.com Ⓛ 10.00–18.00, closed Mon), housing vestiges of earlier civilisations, from Gallo-Roman to the 19th century. They were first discovered during excavations in the 1960s. The largest structure of its type in the world, it extends 118 m (387 ft). ❷ 6 Parvis-de-Notre-Dame, Île de la Cité, 4th Ⓦ www.monum.fr & www.cathedraledeparis.com Ⓛ Tower 10.00–18.00 Tues–Sun, Cathedral 08.00–18.45 Mon–Sat, 08.00–19.45 Sun Ⓝ Metro: St-Michel or Cité

Opéra Bastille

Designed by Carlos Ott and opened in 1989 for the bicentenary of the French Revolution, the curved, glass-fronted Opéra Bastille has transformed the face of the Bastille district. A full programme of opera and dance is available throughout the year (except August). The building is known for its excellent acoustics – all the better to hear the singers' *bel canto*. ❸ pl. de la Bastille, 12th ❶ 0892 89 90 90 Ⓦ www.opera-de-paris.fr Ⓝ Metro: Bastille

Parc des Buttes Chaumont

This charming park perched above an eastern Parisian hill in the 19th *arrondissement* has artificial rivers, caves and cascades, as well as a folly in shape of a Greco-Roman temple. It was built to encourage relaxation and kids will love the ducks, Punch and Judy puppet show and the pony rides! Ⓛ 07.00–21.00 (23.00 in summer) Ⓝ Metro: Botzaris or Buttes Chaumont

Parc de la Villette

Park, concert venue, cultural complex, La Villette is all these rolled into one lively, entertaining destination. The 28-ha(69-acre) urban park has everything from bamboo grove to sprawling lawns where the open-air cinema festival is held in summer. In the spherical Géode, a huge, hemispheric screen shows compelling documentaries often on nature and the planet. La Villette also includes the Cité des Sciences (see page 89) and the Musée de la Musique (see page 90). ❶ 01 40 03 75 75 ⓦ www.villette.com Ⓜ Metro: Porte de Pantin or Porte de la Villette

Place de la République

Along with the Bastille, the Place de la République is known as a place for partying. A giant bronze statue representing the French Republic stands at its centre. Ⓜ Metro: République

CULTURE

Centre Pompidou

Whatever you may think of the industrial chic look, this is France's most important modern art museum, with such major exhibitions as 'Dada' and 'Los Angeles'. You can see great views from its top floor and the **Georges** restaurant (❶ 01 44 78 47 99 ❶ reservations recommended). On the first Sunday of the month admission to the exhibitions is free. The Place Beaubourg in front of the Centre Pompidou is an animated gathering place, with musicians and other performers amusing the crowds, so you can enjoy this destination even if you don't wish to art-gaze. Tips: to avoid queuing, visit the museum after 17.00. ⓐ pl. Georges Pompidou, 4th ❶ 01 44 78 12 33 ⓦ www.centrepompidou.fr ❶ 11.00–21.00 Wed–Mon, until 23.00 Thur for some temporary exhibitions Ⓜ Metro: Rambuteau

⬥ The funky Georges restaurant at Centre Pompidou

La Cinémathèque Française

This treasure trove of movie history includes an exceptional collection of 40,000 films plus a movie-themed library, exhibition halls and four movie theatres showing classic films from all types of cinema year-round. ⓐ 51 rue de Bercy, Parc de Bercy, 12th ⓣ 01 71 19 33 33 ⓦ www.cinematheque.fr ⓛ 12.00–19.00 Mon, Wed & Fri, 12.00–22.00 Thur, 10.00–20.00 Sat & Sun ⓜ Metro: Bercy

⬥ *The eye-catching science museum*

NIGHT VIEWS

All of the Seine's bridges are illuminated at night, so anywhere you walk along the river you get that quintessential romantic Paris perspective. Diners at the Bistro Marguerite (see page 95) get splendid night views of the Seine right across the street, with perhaps the moon lighting the scene from above. Across the Place de l'Hôtel de Ville, the grand town hall is spotlit at night and glows beside the Seine.

Cité des Sciences

Part of the Parc de la Villette, the Cité des Sciences hosts interesting exhibitions connected with inventions and human behaviour. Interactive exhibits cover Earth matters from volcanoes to oceans. There is also a planetarium and 3-D cinema. ❹ 30 av. Corentin-Cariou, 11th ❶ 01 40 05 70 00 ❿ www.cite-sciences.fr ❺ 10.00–18.00, until 19.00 Sun, closed Mon ❷ Metro: Porte de la Villette

Maison Européenne de la Photographie

This gallery supports major contemporary figures working in exhibition prints, the printed page and film. ❹ 5–7 rue de Fourcy, 4th ❶ 01 44 78 75 00 ❺ 11.00–20.00 Wed–Sun ❷ Metro: St-Paul or Pont Marie

Musée des Arts et Métiers

This fascinating museum dedicated to inventions and technology from the 16th century to today houses some 80,000 objects. Exhibits include steam-powered vehicles, such as Cugnot's Fardier, and planes flown by Blériot and Ader. The building, an ancient priory, is particularly appealing. Even the metro station is inventive (on line 11 only, not line 3), resembling the inside of a copper-toned submarine. ⓐ 60 rue Réaumur, 2nd ❶ 01 53 01 82 00 Ⓦ www.arts-et-metiers.net 🕙 10.00–18.00, until 21.30 Thur, closed Mon Ⓝ Metro: Arts et Métiers

Musée de la Musique

Featuring a 900-year history of musical instruments, the museum is part of the Cité de la Musique, which houses several concert halls, a music school and the Paris Conservatoire in the Parc de la Villette. It displays scale models of musical venues and opera houses as well as instrument collections dating back to the Middle Ages. ⓐ 221 av. Jean Jaurès, 19th ❶ 01 44 84 44 84 Ⓦ www.cite-musique.fr 🕙 12.00–18.00 Tues–Sat, 10.00–18.00 Sun Ⓝ Metro: Porte de Pantin

Musée Picasso

Located in the beautiful 17th-century Hôtel Salé, this is the largest collection of Picasso's paintings, sculptures and photographs under one roof. The museum affords a wonderful opportunity for fans to see so many of the artist's works assembled together, as well as his collection of paintings by Matisse, Renoir and Cézanne. On the first Sunday of the month admission is free. ⓐ 5 rue de Thorigny, 4th ❶ 01 42 71 25 21 Ⓦ www.musee-picasso.fr 🕙 09.30–18.00 (summer); 09.30–17.30 (winter), closed Tues, 1 Jan, 25 Dec Ⓝ Metro: St-Paul

RETAIL THERAPY

Alternatives This tiny boutique in the Marais features couture cast-offs (mainly for men) from such designers as Gucci, Issy Miyake and Jean-Paul Gaultier. ⓐ 18 rue du Roi-de-Sicile, 4th ❶ 01 42 78 31 50 🕙 13.00–18.30 Tues–Sat Ⓝ Metro: St-Paul

○ *Try shopping for women's clothes here*

Antoine & Lili Local clothing designers have created a hit line of reasonably priced clothes and accessories for women in Antoine & Lili. Stores in bright pinks, yellows and greens are cheerful and fun. Several locations around Paris. ⓐ 95 quai de Valmy, 51 rue des Francs-Bourgeois, 4th ⓣ 01 42 72 26 60 ⓦ www.antoineetlili.com Ⓝ Metro: Hôtel de Ville

Bercy Village Shopping, dining and relaxing in a riverside atmosphere are all here at the Cour Saint-Emilion in Bercy Village. This is not just a commercial venture. People live in this engaging complex that was once the world's largest wine market. There is even a bakery school. Club Med runs restaurants and a nightclub here (see page 97). ⓐ rue François Truffaut, 12th ⓣ 01 40 02 90 80 ⓦ www.bercyvillage.com Ⓝ Metro: Cour Saint-Emilion

🔺 *A great choice of bird boxes at the lively Sunday bird market*

Concept Nature A conveniently located African shop with decorative items from Togo, Ghana, Mali, Congo and Kenya, Concept Nature features gift and household items, including candleholders, lamps, carved chairs and bowls and traditional African instruments.
🅐 28 rue de Rivoli, 1st 📞 01 42 77 11 19 Ⓜ Metro: St-Paul

CSAO The spacious Compagnie de Senegal et de l'Afrique de l'Ouest reflects Paris's rich African population, promoting the best of Senegal in this cheerful shop with its 'sustainably minded' accessories and trinkets. Bright little plastic bracelets resembling beaded bangles are a modern version of the old elephant hair bracelets Senegalese ladies wore. Rhythmic African CDs, paintings, baskets aplenty, funky furniture from recycled materials and calabash gourd bowls are all sold. ③ 9 rue Elzévir, 3rd ❶ 01 42 71 33 17 ⬤ 11.00–19.00 Mon–Sat, 14.00–19.00 Sun ⓝ Metro: St-Paul

Flower & bird market The flower market is a sight to behold with its array of colourful and aromatic flora. On Sundays, songbirds, cockatoos and other feathered friends are also sold here. ③ pl. Louis-Lepine, Île de la Cité, 4th ⬤ Bird market 08.00–19.00 Sun, Flower market 08.00–19.30 ⓝ Metro: La Cité

Marché de la Création Vendors at Bastille's outdoor market display a wide variety of arts, crafts and also junk. ③ from blvd Quinet to Montparnasse Tower, 15th ⓦ www.marchecreation.com ⬤ 09.00–dusk every Sunday ⓝ Metro: Edgar Quinet

Viaduc des Arts A renovated train viaduct has metamorphosed into a clutch of craftsmen's shops and showrooms at the Viaduc des Arts. Above is as delightful a surprise as the brick boutiques below. Here, the elevated Promenade Plantée, a flowering footpath linking several gardens, winds nearly 5 km (3 miles) along an old railway line to the Bois de Vincennes. The peaceful urban 'lung' provides a great, unobstructed view of the 12th *arrondissement*. ⓦ www.viaduc-des-arts.com ⓝ Metro: Bastille

TAKING A BREAK

L'Apparemment Café £ ❶ In this cosy café in the Marais near the Picasso Museum, patrons play chess and relax. Sunday is *journée brunch*. ③ 18 rue des Coutures Saint-Gervais (off rue de Thorigny), 3rd

☎ 01 48 87 12 22 **⏱** 12.00–14.00 & 16.00–02.00 Sat, 12.30–24.00 Sun
Ⓝ Metro: Filles du Calvaire

Berthillon £ ❷ Even on rainy, cold days there is a queue at
Berthillon, the city's finest ice-cream shop. Choose from more
than 20 exotic flavours. **Ⓐ** 29–31 rue Saint-Louis-en-l'Île, 4th
☎ 01 43 54 31 61 **Ⓦ** www.berthillon.fr **⏱** 10.00–20.00 Wed–Sun
Ⓝ Metro: Pont Marie

Chez Prune £ ❸ A cheerful little bar/restaurant with mango-yellow
walls and a slightly worn look. Staff are very friendly and there's a
lively buzz. **Ⓐ** 71 quai de Valmy, 10th **☎** 01 42 41 30 47 **⏱** 08.00–02.00,
from 10.00 Sun **Ⓝ** Metro: Goncourt or Jacques-Bonsergent

Finkelsztajn's £ ❹ The sign on Sacha Finkelsztajn's window reads
'Gastronomie Europe Centrale et Russie'. Polish immigrants founded
the original store here in 1851, and now two family owned shops sell
such specialities as cheesecake, huge cinnamon-sprinkled apple
strudels and just-baked bread. Deli items include traditional
sausages, dill pickles and salads.
Florence Ⓐ 24 rue des Ecouffes, 4th **☎** 01 48 87 92 85 **⏱** 10.00–19.00,
closed Wed **Ⓝ** Metro: St-Paul
Sacha Ⓐ 27 rue des Rosiers, 4th **☎** 01 42 72 78 91 **⏱** 10.00–19.00
Wed–Mon, closed mid-July–mid-Aug **Ⓝ** Metro: St-Paul

Le Baba Bourgeois £–££ ❺ Enjoy a good brunch and a great view
at this 1970s Italian-designed restaurant. **Ⓐ** 5 quai de la Tournelle,
4th **☎** 01 44 07 46 75 **Ⓦ** www.lebababourgeois.com **⏱** Brunch
11.30–17.00 Sat & Sun, Restaurant 11.00–23.30 Tues–Sat
Ⓝ Metro: Pont Marie

AFTER DARK

RESTAURANTS

Le Bistro Marguerite £ ❻ This Seine-side gem, with its view of the Hôtel de Ville and riverside setting, is a typical French bistro with a rustic, country décor, friendly staff and reasonable prices. Choices include such traditional French fare as *aligot* (puréed cheese and garlic potatoes) and tender pork knuckle. Also open for breakfast and lunch.
🅐 2 quai de Gesvres, 4th ❶ 01 42 72 00 04 Ⓝ Metro: Hôtel de Ville

Les Bas-Fonds £–££ ❼ Restaurant and *bar à vin*. Let the wine steward take charge while you relax in a cosy and candle-lit atmosphere.
🅐 116 rue Amelot, 11th ❶ 01 48 05 00 30 Ⓦ www.lesbasfonds.com
🕒 12.00–15.00 Mon–Fri, 19.00–23.30 Ⓝ Metro: Filles du Calvaire

Le Coude Fou £–££ ❽ With its naïve paintings on the walls and ceiling, this quirky wine bar/restaurant serves good, typically French food with a wide choice of wines. 🅐 12 rue du Bourg-Tibourg (off rue de Rivoli), 4th ❶ 01 42 77 15 16 🕒 12.00–14.00 & 19.00–24.00
Ⓝ Metro: Hôtel de Ville

Café de l'Industrie ££ ❾ This restaurant attracts a youthful crowd with its good food at reasonable prices. Lamb *noisettes* and fresh fish are typical menu items. Staff are young and enthusiastic and décor is 'anthropological', with old colonial outpost photos, masks and fan palms. 🅐 16 & 17 rue Saint-Sabin, 11th ❶ 01 47 00 13 53
🕒 10.00–02.00 Ⓝ Metro: Bastille

La Tête Ailleurs ££ ❿ In an old building in the Marais, this restaurant has been gentrified to provide a warm, Provençal farmhouse atmosphere.

The food is excellent and the service friendly. ③ 20 rue Beautreillis, 4th
① 01 42 72 47 80 ⑩ www.lateteailleurs-restaurant-paris.com
⑤ 12.00–14.00 & 20.00–22.30 Mon–Fri, 20.00–22.30 Sat,
closed 2 weeks in Aug ⑩ Metro: St-Paul

Le Train Bleu £££ (set menu) **£££** (à la carte) ⑪ With its belle époque
ceiling hung with chandeliers and painted with scenes of Paris and
other cities, this grand restaurant and its Big Ben Bar evoke a gentler
age. Situated above the Gare de Lyon, which was built for the 1900
World Fair, the dining room is the best-preserved part of the original
building. The restaurant attracts a mixed clientele: young locals,
travellers and older Parisians. As its brochure says, outside in the
modern world, 'linear design has triumphed over the curves of
Baroque art'. Even if you don't wish to have a drink or a meal,

◐ *The opulent Le Train Blue above the Gare de Lyon*

it is worth popping your head in to catch a glimpse of this splendid setting. ⓐ Gare de Lyon, pl. Louis Armand, 12th ❶ 01 44 75 76 76 ⓦ www.le-train-bleu.com ⓝ Metro: Gare de Lyon

BARS, CLUBS & ENTERTAINMENT

Bercy Live concerts are held just about every night here, with a whole range of music, including jazz, rock, hip-hop and rhythm-and-blues. ⓐ 12 blvd du Bercy, 12th ❶ 01 40 02 60 60 ⓦ www.bercy.fr ⓝ Metro: Bercy

Club Med World A complex run by the famous French resort group, which includes two restaurants and two bar/discos. ⓐ 39 cour St-Emilion, Bercy, 12th ❶ 08 10 81 04 10 ⓦ www.clubmedworld.fr ⓛ 11.00–02.00 Tues–Thur, 11.00–06.00 Fri & Sat, 11.00–08.00 Sun ⓝ Metro: Bercy

Flèche d'Or Café This cavernous space, in a former train station, is popular for its live bands. Music ranges from Afro and reggae to rock, jazz and rhythm-and-blues, among other genres. You have to queue to get in, and you take your chances with the music. ⓐ 102 bis rue de Bagnolet, 20th ❶ 01 44 64 01 02 ⓦ www.flechedor.fr ⓝ Metro: Alexandre Dumas or Gambetta

New Morning A former printing shop, this Paris institution is known for its concerts of jazz and world music. ⓐ 7–9 rue des Petites-Ecuries, 10th ❶ 01 45 23 51 41 ⓦ www.newmorning.com ⓛ 20.00–24.00 Mon–Sat ⓝ Metro: Château d'Eau

OPA This nightclub offers free entry to live music, electro, rock and other sounds. ⓐ 9 rue Biscornet, 12th ❶ 01 46 28 12 90 ⓦ www.opa-paris.com ⓛ 20.00–06.00 ⓝ Metro: Bastille

Left Bank

The Left Bank is the Paris of universities and bohemia, of literary cafés, student hangouts and artists' *ateliers* and galleries. Such historically important buildings as the Sorbonne, the Panthéon, the Eiffel Tower and the Musée d'Orsay are all found here. Although they are located on islands in the Seine, Notre-Dame and the Conciergerie are actually in the 1st *arrondissement*, and so are listed under the Right Bank. Called the *Rive Gauche* in French, the large and varied Left Bank of Paris includes the legendary Latin Quarter in the 5th *arrondissement*, the more bourgeois 7th, where the Eiffel Tower and Invalides stand, and the soaring Tour Montparnasse in the 15th.

SIGHTS & ATTRACTIONS

Boulevard St-Germain
While the Champs-Élysées is the grand thoroughfare of the Right Bank, Saint-Germain is the main boulevard of the Left, where boutiques and bistros, cafés and cinemas, street entertainers and *flâneurs* (strollers) all converge. It is also known for its little jazz joints and art galleries on side streets such as rue de Seine, rue des Beaux-Arts and rue Bonaparte.

Église Saint-Sulpice
This fine church is noted for its paintings by Eugène Delacroix (first chapel on the right as you enter) and for its organ. The fountain square in front is a popular place to rest and often has an outdoor photo exhibition ❸ pl. Saint-Sulpice, 6th ❶ 01 46 33 21 78 Ⓦ www.paroisse-saint-sulpice-paris.org ❻ 07.30–19.30 Ⓝ Metro: Saint-Sulpice

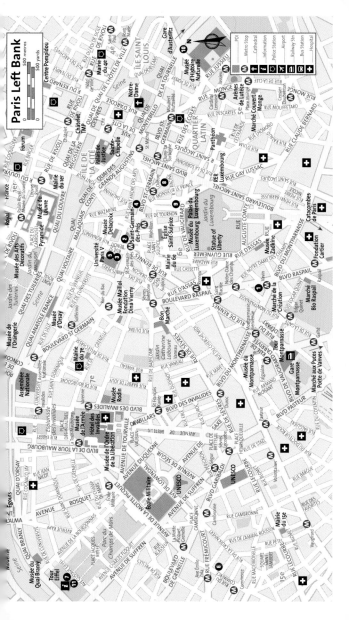

Hôtel des Invalides

Recognisable for its gold-leaf dome shining brilliantly along
the Left Bank horizon, the Hôtel des Invalides is where Napoleon
is buried. His ashes are protected in a sarcophagus containing
six coffins, of iron, lead and wood. One of the most beautiful
17th-century monuments in Paris, Les Invalides was built during
the time of Louis XIV to house wounded soldiers. Parts of it are
still used as a hospital. There are five museums here, including
the Musée de l'Armée. Its Cathédrale Saint-Louis occasionally
has classical music concerts. ⓐ esplanade des Invalides, 7th
ⓣ 01 44 42 38 77 ⓦ www.invalides.org ⓛ 10.00–18.00 (summer),
(19.00 for the dome); 10.00–17.00 (winter) Ⓝ Metro: Invalides

Jardin du Luxembourg

Adjacent to the Senate building, this is a true Parisian park, with an
orderly French garden, tree-lined alleys, green spaces, statues and
bassins (ponds), around which Parisians sit on fine days. The *guignol*
(a puppet theatre) entertains children as it has done for centuries.
You can watch regulars playing *boules*, bridge and chess, or just
hang out like the locals, lounging on the metal chairs watching
children sail miniature boats on the ornamental pond. A hidden
charm in the west side of the Jardin du Luxembourg is the bronze
model of the Statue of Liberty, which the sculptor Auguste Bartholdi
gave to the garden in 1900 for the World Fair. Bartholdi, who sculpted
the full-sized Statue of Liberty that now stands in New York harbour,
based his masterpiece on this model and a larger one that fronts
the Pont de Grenelle in the Seine. ⓐ rue de Vaugirard, 6th
ⓛ sunrise–sunset Ⓝ RER B: Luxembourg

● *The striking Hôtel des Invalides is the burial site of Napoleon*

Jardin des Plantes

Part of the natural history museum (see page 108) and dating back to a 17th-century medicinal garden, the Jardin des Plantes has one of the most beautiful rose gardens in Paris, with some 350 varieties. There are also alpine and tropical gardens, medicinal plants, as well as a micro-zoo and menagerie. ⓐ entrance on rue Cuvier, 5th ⓛ 08.00–18.00 (summer); 08.00–17.00 (winter) Ⓜ Metro: Jussieu

Markets

Paris's markets are an attraction in themselves, reminiscent of the traditional form of country commerce, where vendors call out their wares to passers-by and goods range from fresh, tempting foodstuffs to books, birds and collectables.

Marché Bio Raspail Organic food market. ⓐ blvd Raspail between rue du Cherche-Midi and rue de Rennes, 6th ⓛ 09.00–15.00 Sun Ⓜ Metro: Rennes

Marché Couvert Monge At this covered food market in the Latin Quarter, vocal vendors sell a wide range of produce, meat, cheese and delicacies. ⓐ pl. Monge, 5th ⓛ 07.00–14.30 Wed–Fri, 07.00–15.00 Sun Ⓜ Metro: Place Monge

Marché aux Puces de la Porte de Vanves Past the polyester clothing stalls and oddball junk, you can find some gems at this flea market, such as lace fabrics, antique tables and silverware. ⓐ av. de la Porte de Vanves & av. Marc Sangnier, 14th ⓣ 06 86 89 99 96 ⓦ www.pucesdeparis-portedevanves.com ⓛ 07.00–19.30 Sat & Sun Ⓜ Metro: Porte de Vanves

Odéon

The Odéon district of boulevard Saint-Germain is always full of students, shoppers and movie-goers (there are several major cinema complexes here). Shops range from couture to little boutiques and there are also theatres, bookstores and cafés, including Paris's oldest café, Le Procope (see page 115). Ⓜ Metro: Odéon

Panthéon

One of the most recognised of Paris monuments is the Panthéon, in the 5th *arrondissement*. Since 1791, this stately, domed structure has been the revered resting place of some of France's most eminent figures, including Voltaire, Victor Hugo, Jean-Jacques Rousseau, Emile Zola, Marie Curie and a recent inductee, Alexandre Dumas. Tours of the nave and crypt are available. A fascinating permanent exhibit is that of Foucault's pendulum, which hangs from high above in the dome's crown and swings slowly and hypnotically by observers near the Panthéon floor. ❷ pl. du Panthéon ❶ Guided visits in English 01 44 54 19 30 Ⓦ www.monum.fr Ⓛ 10.00–18.30 (summer); 10.00–18.00 (winter) Ⓜ Metro: Cardinal Lemoine

Quartier Latin (Latin Quarter)

So-named because the students and teachers of the Sorbonne spoke Latin until the French Revolution (1789), the Latin Quarter in the 5th *arrondissement* has long been associated with students, writers and intellectuals. It has now expanded beyond a centre of learning to become a *quartier* of cafés and bars, boutiques, bistros and nightspots. The area includes the lively Saint-Michel warren of cobbled streets and restaurants, the Sorbonne, the Panthéon and the medieval Cluny museum. Bustling and narrow, rue Mouffetard is one of the city's oldest streets; it was the main road from Paris (then called Lutèce) to Rome in ancient times. 'Le Mouff' has a lively weekend market, little boutiques and reasonably priced restaurants. There is even a Roman arena, the **Arènes de Lutèce** (❷ 47 rue Monge, 5th

🕒 08.00–22.00 (summer); 08.00–17.30 (winter) Ⓜ Metro: Place Monge), an admission-free Gallo-Roman ruin, which was once a circus amphitheatre.

Saint-Germain-des-Prés

This Romanesque church on the boulevard bearing its name has the oldest belfry in Paris. Inside it is very peaceful, a wonderful place to ponder. On the corner of the boulevard Saint-Germain-des-Prés are the legendary literary cafés Les Deux Magots and Café de Flore (see pages 113–14). Ⓜ Metro: Saint-Germain-des-Prés

Seine

The city was first settled on an island (the Île de la Cité) on the Seine, and the river remains one of its most appealing and vital features. Many of the city's finest attractions are found along its banks: the Louvre, Musée d'Orsay, the Eiffel Tower, Notre-Dame and the Conciergerie. The Seine can be appreciated on a stroll along its quays with its 37 distinctive bridges, or from one of the many cruise boats. Especially romantic are night-time dinner cruises.

Bâteaux Parisiens depart from the foot of the Eiffel Tower hourly from 10.00 to 23.00 (until 22.00 in winter). Lunch and dinner cruises are also available. ☎ 01 46 99 43 13 🌐 www.bateauxparisiens.com

Batobus, a regular boat service making eight stops along the Seine, is like an inexpensive cruise, without the commentary. Service operates year-round except January and gives great views of some of Paris's most famous buildings. ☎ 08 25 05 01 01 🌐 www.batobus.com

◀ *Ornate gold statues adorn the Pont Alexandre on the River Seine*

Tour Eiffel (Eiffel Tower)

Gustave Eiffel built Paris's most visible and well-known site and the international symbol of France, the graceful Tour Eiffel, for the 1889 World Fair. When it was first assembled, the tower was widely disparaged. Parisians called it a pitiful lamppost and a hollow candlestick. Today, the French, and visitors from around the world, admire the filigreed, A-shaped structure above the Seine. At 324 m high (1,063 ft), the tower has 1,665 steps and requires some 50 tonnes of paint to repaint it in 'Tour Eiffel Brown'. Twenty thousand light bulbs light it like a birthday sparkler each hour after dark until 01.00. There are lifts to the three levels, which cost more the higher you go.
ⓐ Champs-de-Mars, 7th ⓣ 01 44 11 23 23 ⓦ www.tour-eiffel.fr
ⓛ 09.30–23.00 (last lift for the top 22.30); 09.00–24.00 mid-June–end Aug ⓝ Metro: Bir-Hakeim

Tour Montparnasse

Although it is a black blight on the Paris skyline, the Tour Montparnasse redeems itself through its spectacular view from the 56th floor. It has a 210-m (689-ft) terrace and café, the loftiest in Paris and the ideal place to drink in (or to) the spectacular views. ⓐ rue de l'Arrivée, 15th
ⓣ 01 45 38 52 56 ⓦ www.tourmontparnasse56.com ⓛ 09.30–23.30 Apr–Sept (last lift leaves half an hour before closing)
ⓝ Metro: Montparnasse-Bienvenüe

CULTURE

Les Catacombes de Paris

The Catacombs came about when the Cimetière des Innocents became a threat to public health. All the bones were collected and transferred into this ossuary, which can still send a shiver up your

🔺 *The Eiffel Tower stands tall above Paris*

vertebrae. Ⓐ 1 av. du Colonel Henri Rol-Tanguy, 14th Ⓣ 01 42 23 47 63
Ⓛ 10.00–17.00 Tues–Sun Ⓝ Metro: Denfert-Rochereau

Fondation Cartier

The Fondation Cartier, established in 1984, is a private foundation
for contemporary art. Huge windows let in the natural light, while
outside grounds filled with tall trees emphasise the height of the
display space and give a sense of bringing the outdoors in. Exhibitions
focus on individual artists or themes from design to photography,
painting to video. Ⓐ 261 blvd Raspail, 6th Ⓣ 01 42 18 56 50
Ⓦ www.fondation.cartier.com Ⓛ 12.00–20.00 Tues–Sun,
22.00 on Tues Ⓝ Metro: Raspail

Musée Delacroix

The painter's last home and *atelier* is now a charming, intimate
museum, with displays of his work as well as memorabilia and letters
to friends such as Charles Baudelaire and Georges Sand. Admission
is free on the first Sunday of the month. Ⓐ 6 rue de Furstenberg, 6th
Ⓣ 01 44 41 86 50 Ⓦ www.musee-delacroix.fr Ⓛ 09.30–17.00 Wed–Mon
Ⓝ Metro: Saint-Germain-des-Prés or Mabillon

Musée d'Histoire Naturelle

It's Jurassic Park without the violence at this natural history
museum, where you can see reconstructions of dinosaurs, African
game such as giraffes, and marine species. The evolution gallery,
with its extinct and threatened section, makes you realise what we
need to protect and preserve. Ⓐ Jardin des Plantes, 36 rue Geoffroy
Saint-Hilaire, 5th Ⓣ 01 40 79 56 01 Ⓦ www.mnhn.fr Ⓛ 10.00–18.00
Wed–Mon (summer); 10.00–17.00 (winter) Ⓝ Metro: Jussieu

Musée du Luxembourg

Some of the city's most important visiting exhibitions are held in the former orangery of the Senate building in the Jardin du Luxembourg. ➋ 19 rue de Vaugirard, 6th ➊ 01 42 34 25 95, Reservations 08 92 68 46 94 Ⓦ www.museeduluxembourg.fr, Reservations www.billet-coupe-file.com ➐ 10.30–19.00 Tues–Thur & Sat, 10.30–22.00 Mon & Fri, 09.00–19.00 Sun Ⓝ RER B: Luxembourg

Musée Maillol Fondation Dina Vierny

This museum displays works by Maillol, including sculptures and paintings, as well as works from the private collection of Dina Vierny, such as those by Matisse, Gauguin, Rousseau and Kandinsky. It also holds temporary exhibitions of such well-known artists as Duffy and Fernando Botero. The charming, barrel-vaulted café in the basement serves drinks and snacks. ➋ 59 rue de Grenelle, 7th ➊ 01 42 22 59 58 Ⓦ www.museemaillol.com ➐ 11.00–18.00 Wed–Mon, closed holidays Ⓝ Metro: Rue du Bac

Musée du Montparnasse

Visiting this museum is like stepping back in time to 19th-century Paris. The entrance into this charming former painter's studio/canteen is via a peaceful cobbled alleyway. ➋ 21 av. du Maine, 14th ➊ 01 42 22 91 96 Ⓦ www.museedumontparnasse.net ➐ 12.30–19.00 Tues–Sun Ⓝ Metro: Montparnasse-Bienvenüe

Musée d'Orsay

More than a museum, this grand structure, built as a train station for the World Fair in 1900, is an attraction in itself. The light-filled rooms and lofty, luminous central gallery set off some of the world's greatest artworks to their best advantage. The permanent collection

◓ *The intricate beauty of the Musée d'Orsay clock*

encompasses the whole range of fine arts from the mid-19th century to the early 20th. The upper floor is devoted to Impressionists and Post-Impressionists, with famous works by Monet, Renoir, Degas, Cézanne, Pissarro, Sisley and Van Gogh. As well as the permanent collections, there are always rotating exhibitions. In summer, the open-air terrace on level five gives a fabulous view of the Seine and all the historic riverfront buildings. Admission to the museum is free on the first Sunday of the month.

The Passerelle de Solferino pedestrian bridge across the Seine links the Musée d'Orsay in a graceful steel arch with the Jardin des Tuileries on the Right Bank. ⓐ 1 rue de la Légion d'Honneur, 7th ⓣ 01 40 49 48 14 ⓦ www.musee-orsay.fr ⓛ 09.30–18.00 Tues–Sat, 10.00–21.45 Thur, 09.30–18.00 Sun ⓜ Metro: Solférino

Musée du Quai Branly

This museum along the Seine next to the Eiffel Tower houses arts and artefacts from the civilisations of Africa, Asia, Oceania and the Americas. Among its collections are items moved from the Musée de l'Homme and the Musée des Arts d'Afrique et d'Océanie. ⓐ 55 quai Branly, 7th ⓣ 01 56 61 70 00 ⓦ www.quaibranly.fr ⓛ 10.00–18.30 Tues–Sun, 21.30 Thur ⓜ Metro: léna

Musée Rodin

The Musée Rodin provides a pleasant, green escape in the heart of Paris. Housed in a delightful 18th-century mansion, the museum contains bronze and marble work by Auguste Rodin (1840–1917), as well as works by Van Gogh, Monet, Renoir and others. Famous works such as *The Thinker*, *The Kiss* and *Eve* are scattered through the garden, which may be visited separately. ⓐ 79 rue de Varenne, 7th ⓣ 01 44 18 61 10 ⓦ www.musee-rodin.fr ⓛ 09.30–17.45 (summer);

9.30–16.45 (winter) Ⓝ Metro: Varenne ❶ Last entrance half an hour before closing

Musée Zadkine

The Russian artist Ossip Zadkine bequeathed his home and garden to the city of Paris. Some 100 of his works here include distinctive sculptures of bronze and tree trunks. ⓐ 100 bis rue d'Assas, 6th ❶ 01 55 42 77 20 Ⓦ www.paris.fr ❶ 10.00–18.00 Tues–Sun, closed public holidays Ⓝ RER B: Port-Royal; metro: Notre-Dame-des-Champs or Vavin

RETAIL THERAPY

La Bagagerie These stores sell all kinds of bags, from little clutches and practical office totes to wheeled suitcases. Prices are reasonable and staff friendly. Several locations, including ⓐ 41 rue du Four, 6th ❶ 01 45 48 85 88 Ⓦ www.labagagerie.com ❶ 10.15–19.00 Ⓝ Metro: Mabillon

Le Bon Marché The oldest department store in Paris is nonetheless *très chic*, known for its ready-to-wear items, household goods and La Grande Epicerie (at no. 38), with some 5,000 of the world's finest foodstuffs. Some of the little streets around Le Bon Marché, such as rue de l'Abbé Grégoire and rue Saint-Placide, often have sales and low prices. ⓐ 24 rue de Sèvres, 6th ❶ 01 44 39 80 00 Ⓦ www.lebonmarche.fr ❶ 09.30–19.00 Mon–Fri, until 21.00 Thur, 09.30–20.00 Sat Ⓝ Metro: Sèvres-Babylone

Debauve et Gallais In 1800, Louis XVI's personal pharmacists founded this store, which is now a famous *chocolatier*. ⓐ 30 rue des Saints-Pères, 6th ❶ 01 45 48 54 67 Ⓦ www.debauve-et-gallais.com ❶ 09.30–19.00 Mon–Sat Ⓝ Metro: Saint-Germain-des-Prés

Les Filles à la Vanille With three outlets on the Left Bank, Les Filles à la Vanille stocks clothes, accessories and bags for women. ⓐ 1 rue de l'Ancienne Comédie (corner of rue de Buci, off pl Henri Mondor), 6th ⓛ 10.00–19.00 Mon–Sat ⓣ 01 43 26 61 66 ⓝ Metro: Odéon

La Maison Ivre This small boutique sells distinctive Provençal ceramics with jugs, bowls, tiles and other items coloured in the warm hues of the Mediterranean. ⓐ 38 rue Jacob, 6th ⓣ 01 42 60 01 85 ⓛ 10.30–19.00 Mon–Sat ⓝ Metro: Saint-Germain-des-Prés

Zadig & Voltaire Designer jeans, bags and t-shirts, some affordable, by such creators as Helmut Lang and Yoshi Nagasawa. Several locations, including ⓐ 1 rue du Vieux-Colombier, 6th ⓣ 01 43 29 18 29 ⓝ Metro: Saint-Sulpice

TAKING A BREAK

La Coupole £ ❶ This famous 1900s brasserie in Montparnasse has rotating artwork displays, such as portraits of celebrated patrons of the past (like Hemingway and Jean-Paul Sartre). It is open for full meals, but for a light snack, the '*Formule Thé*' includes a tasty pastry, such as a seasonal fruit tart, and tea, delicious hot chocolate or coffee. ⓐ 102 blvd du Montparnasse, 6th ⓣ 01 43 20 14 20 ⓛ 08.00–01.00 Mon–Fri, 08.30–01.30 Sat & Sun ⓝ Metro: Vavin

Les Deux Magots & Café de Flore £ ❷ & ❸ Since the late 19th/early 20th century, these two famous cafés on boulevard Saint-Germain have welcomed writers, artists and intellectuals, including Trotsky, Hemingway, Camus, Sartre and Simone de Beauvoir. Today, both sponsor writers' prizes to keep up the literary tradition.

Les Deux Magots has comfy wooden chairs, polished glass and brass, waiters in bow ties, black suits and long white aprons, and a view of the tower of the Saint-Germain-des-Prés church. English newspapers are available. ❷ 6 pl. Saint-Germain-des-Prés, 6th ❶ 01 45 48 55 25 🕒 07.30–01.00 Ⓜ Metro: Saint-Germain-des-Prés

Café de Flore is just as charming, and the hot chocolate here, served in a Flore-engraved silver jug, equals that of the neighbouring Deux Magots. ❷ 172 blvd Saint-Germain, 6th ❶ 01 45 48 55 26 🕒 07.00–01.00 Ⓜ Metro: Saint-Germain-des-Prés

⬇ *Quintessential Parisian café*

Le Procope £ ❹ Here in the oldest café in Paris (1686), Diderot and d'Alembert began compiling their encyclopaedia in 1727. Le Procope is known for its *cuisine traditionnelle*. ❷ 13 rue de l'Ancienne Comédie (off pl Henri Mondor), 6th ❶ 01 40 46 79 00 ❶ until 01.00 ❶ Metro: Odéon

AFTER DARK

RESTAURANTS

La Brasserie Saint Benoît £ ❺ Good traditional French fare, often with a complimentary kir, is served in this simple restaurant in the Saint-Germain district. ❷ 26 rue Saint Benoît, 6th ❶ 01 45 48 29 66 ❶ 12.00–14.30 & 18.00–midnight, closed Sun lunch ❶ Metro: Saint-Germain-des-Prés

Café du Commerce £ ❻ The historic café is spread over three levels around an atrium hung with cascading vines with a décor that evokes an earlier era. With starters such as excellent *salade chèvre chaud* (hot goat's cheese salad) and varied main courses such as grilled pork knuckle, steak with pepper sauce or fish of the day, the Commerce is excellent value. ❷ 51 rue du Commerce, 15th ❶ 01 45 75 03 27 ❶ 12.00–15.00 & 19.00–24.00 ❶ Metro: Avenue Émile Zola or Commerce

Altitude 95 £–££ ❼ If prices in the Jules Verne (see page 116) are too stratospheric, the Altitude 95 (95 m above sea level) is reasonably priced and has a pretty panoramic view, too. ❷ Level One, Eiffel Tower, 7th ❶ 01 45 55 20 04 ❶ 12.00–24.00 ❶ Metro: Bir-Hakeim

Le Bouillon Racine £–££ ❽ In this art nouveau-style restaurant you can enjoy traditional meals. Belgian beer is accompanied by really good value for money dishes. ❷ 3 rue Racine, 6th ❶ 01 44 32 15 60

www.bouillon-racine.com 12.00–01.00
Metro: Cluny-La Sorbonne

Au Gourmand £–££ This restaurant, across the street from the Luxembourg garden and just a block from the Musée du Luxembourg, offers elegant fare at reasonable prices. The menu includes a variety of seafood dishes and roasts, steaks and chops accompanied by excellent truffle mashed potatoes. 22 rue de Vaugirard, 6th 01 43 26 26 45 Lunch Mon–Fri, Dinner Mon–Sat
RER B: Luxembourg

Le Ziryab ££ Known for its couscous and its fabulous view of the Notre-Dame and the Seine, this Moroccan restaurant sits atop the Institut du Monde Arabe (see Multicultural Paris, page 118).
1 rue des Fossés-Saint-Bernard, 5th 01 53 10 10 20 Lunch 12.00–14.30, Tea salon 15.00–18.00, Dinner 18.30–23.00, closed Mon
Metro: Jussieu

Le Jules Verne £££ For high-class, high-altitude (and high-priced) fare, try the 1-star Le Jules Verne restaurant, located on the second level of the Eiffel Tower. The restaurant has its own lift and terrace. Diners have an excellent view of the city stretching along the river.
Level Two, Eiffel Tower, 7th 01 45 55 61 44 12.15–13.45 & 19.15–21.45 Metro: Bir-Hakeim

BARS, CLUBS & ENTERTAINMENT
Le Bar du Marché This fashionable bar painted bright red on the corner of Buci and rue de Seine is *branché* (trendy) by night and great for people-watching on sunny afternoons as a pavement café. Waiters wear overalls, the market vendors' dress code of yore.

Ideal for a sunny breakfast *en terrasse*. ❸ 75 rue de Seine, 6th
❶ 01 43 26 55 15 ❺ 07.30–02.00 Ⓝ Metro: Mabillon

Bâteau Six-Huit The Seine becomes the scene at night in this dance
club. ❸ quai Montebello, 5th Ⓦ www.six-huit.com ❺ 21.00–04.00
Ⓝ Metro: St-Michel

Le Batofar Another buzzing and popular dance club on the Seine.
❸ 11 quai François-Mauriac, 13th Ⓦ www.batofar.org ❺ 20.00–04.00
Tues–Sun Ⓝ Metro: Quai de la Gare

Caveau de la Huchette Located in a basement cellar, this is a jazz
institution in the heart of Saint-Michel. ❸ 5 rue de la Huchette, 5th
❶ 01 43 26 65 05 ❺ from 21.30 Tues–Sun Ⓝ Metro: St-Michel

Gare Montparnasse Watch a night-time phenomenon roll through
the Left Bank every Friday night, when masses of rollerbladers
take over the streets, leaving from the Gare Montparnasse in the
15th *arrondissement* at 22.00 and gliding through Paris until 01.00.
Ⓦ www.pari-roller.com Ⓝ Metro: Montparnasse-Bienvenüe

La Mezzanine de l'Alcazar The Mezzanine bar of the Alcazar restaurant
is lively with DJs or pop/rock singers, creating a great ambience for
a drink or a dance. ❸ 62 rue Mazarine, 6th ❶ 01 53 10 19 99
Ⓦ www.alcazar.fr ❺ 19.00–02.00 Ⓝ Metro: Odéon

NIGHT VIEWS

The **Musée National du Moyen Age** in the Hôtel de Cluny is impressive
enough by day, with its medieval artefacts and tapestries, but spotlit
at night (seen along boulevard Saint-Michel) this ancient building

MULTICULTURAL PARIS

Visitors to Paris can only benefit from the city's increasingly multi-ethnic makeup as new and varied influences broaden the cultural range of what it has to offer.

In the last 50 years or so, immigrants from France's former colonies in Algeria, Morocco and West Africa, as well as those from China, the Caribbean and Eastern Europe, have made Paris their home. This infusion of cultures has brought with it a whole new selection of intriguing museums and galleries, shops selling goods from around the world, and a fine collection of restaurants serving foreign cuisine.

Some *quartiers* have a varied mix: in the culturally diverse Belleville area in the north, there are Thai and Vietnamese restaurants, Turkish cafés, Arab grocery stores and kosher butchers. Ménilmontant, east of République, is a neighbourhood of couscous and tagine restaurants competing with those serving Senegalese cuisine.

Generally, though, individual ethnic groups have settled in well-defined areas such as the predominantly North African Goutte d'Or in the 18th *arrondissement* and the Cambodian, Vietnamese, Laotian and Chinese sections of the 13th. The main Jewish community is based around the rue des Rosiers in the Marais, with its delicatessens and restaurants.

'Little India' in the 10th *arrondissement* started out in the 1970s as a couple of shops in a covered arcade, Passage Brady. Now, the area is full of grocers and stores selling traditional Indian saris and incense. Curry restaurants have spread out right across the neighbourhood.

The area around the Barbès-Rochechouart metro station is a West African and West Indian neighbourhood, and a great place to buy dazzling dresses or browse in food markets that sell tropical produce and exotic spices.

Arab culture is officially centred around the beautiful Institut du Monde Arabe (Institute of the Arab World). The 1,600 exterior panels covering its south façade adjust automatically according to sunlight to create a peaceful, reflective atmosphere. Beside the museum's extensive displays of Arab culture, the Institut has a library, a shop, a tea salon serving the city's best mint tea, and a rooftop terrace and restaurant that has a superb view of the Seine and Notre-Dame.

Chinatown, near the Place d'Italie metro station, is as much Southeast Asian as it is Chinese. Giant supermarkets such as Tangs Frères sell every conceivable delicacy of the East, including *galangal*, fish paste, dried lemongrass, chunks of tamarind, and fresh Chinese vegetables such as *bok choy*. Here, Chinese silk dresses and other Asian clothes are sold at discount prices. Other stores in the area sell a variety of Asian home goods and decorations, including Chinese kitchenware, plastic chopsticks, paper lanterns and wooden Buddha statues. Local restaurants serve Vietnamese *pho*, barbecued duck, noodles and other Asian fast food.

But what of that sometimes ill-appreciated ethnic group, the British ex-pat community? These rarefied creatures can be seen crowding around the shelves of WH Smith in the 1st *arrondissement*, grabbing at copies of *The Sun* and *Nuts* and going misty-eyed at the thought of the old country.

Institut du Monde Arabe 🅐 1 rue des Fossés-St-Bernard, 5th
🅣 01 40 51 38 38 🅦 www.imarabe.org 🅛 10.00–18.00,
closed Mon 🅜 Metro: Jussieu
WH Smith 🅐 248 rue de Rivoli, 1st 🅣 01 44 77 88 99
🅦 www.whsmith.fr 🅛 09.00–19.30 Mon–Sat, 13.00–19.30 Sun
🅜 Metro: Concorde

with its Gallo-Roman baths is an awesome, impressive sight in
central Paris. 🅐 6 pl. Paul-Painlevé, 5th 🅜 Metro: Cluny-La Sorbonne

The **Seine** and its bridges and buildings illuminated at night are
a majestic sight.

The **Eiffel Tower** naturally steals the skyline show each night,
when it is bathed in gold and sparkling on the hour, but views from
the top of the **Tour Montparnasse** are also exquisite on a clear night
and well worth the elevator ride to the top (see page 106).

▶ *Medieval masterpiece: the Cathédrale Notre-Dame at Reims*

OUT OF TOWN
trips

Auvers-sur-Oise

For fans of Vincent van Gogh, a visit to the village of Auvers-sur-Oise is a pilgrimage. The artist lived his last two months here, painting some of his most famous works. He took such solace in Auvers that he painted prolifically, producing 78 works during his brief visit. This delightful village – some 30 km (181/2 miles) northwest of Paris – with its stone houses, pretty gardens and cobbled streets remains much as it was in the artist's day, and is still a vibrant artists' community with a number of galleries. The masterpieces painted by Van Gogh and others are indicated throughout by signs called La Mémoire des Lieux, where copies of the paintings are shown at the locations of the scenes painted.

The **Auvers Tourist Office** has brochures, including those of self-guided walks, with maps marking the famous attractions and settings of Van Gogh's works. ⓐ Manoir des Colombières, rue de la Sansonne ❶ 01 30 36 10 06 ❷ 09.30–12.30, 14.00–18.00 (summer) 09.30–12.30, 14.00–17.00 (winter)

GETTING THERE

Take the SNCF train from Gare du Nord or Gare St-Lazare to Pontoise and change for Auvers-sur-Oise (direction Creil). Trains are frequent (every 20–30 minutes) with a total journey time of one hour. During the summer, there are often direct services on a Sunday. An adult return ticket costs €4.

If you're driving, take the A15 in the direction of Cergy-Pontoise, leave the motorway at Exit 7 and take the RN 184 (direction Beauvais) as far as Méry-sur-Oise, then follow the signs for Auvers-sur-Oise.

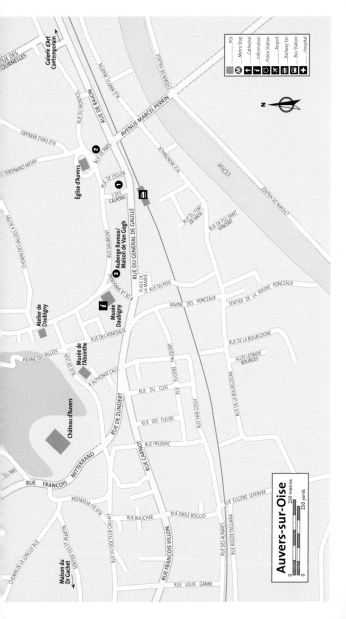

Auvers-sur-Oise

POI
+ Metro Stop
† Cathedral
ℹ Information
🏛 Police Station
✈ Airport
🚉 Railway Stn
🚌 Bus Station
✚ Hospital

N

0   250 metres
0   250 yards

Galerie d'Art Contemporain

Église d'Auvers

❶

❷

Atelier de Daubigny

ℹ Musée Daubigny

❸ Auberge Ravoux/ Maison de Van Gogh

Musée de l'Absinthe

Château d'Auvers

Maison du Dr Gachet

RUE DES TOURNELLES
RUE MARCEL HARTZ
RUE DU MONTCEL
RUE DE PARIS
RUE DE RAJON
RUE ÉMILE BERNARD
FERDINAND MESNY
AVENUE MARCEL PERRIN
CHEMIN DE HALAGE
RUE DE PARIS
RUE DE L'ÉGLISE
S DES CALPONS
CHEMIN DES VALLÉES & BUTRY
RUE DAUBIGNY
RUE DU GÉNÉRAL DE GAULLE
RUE DU FORT DE VAUX
RUE DE RUE SAINT VINCENT
RUE DU REMPART
L'Oise
LOIRE
RAVINE DES VALLÉES
RUE DE LÉRY
RUE DES SAINTS
PLACE DE LA MAIRIE
RUE DU POIS
RAVINE DES PONCEAUX
SENTIER DE LA RAVINE PONCEAUX
RUE DES PONCEAUX
RUE DE LA BOURGOGNE
RUE ALPHONSE CALLÉ
RUE EUGÈNE FALQUERT
RUE DU CLOS
RUE VAN GOGH
ALLÉE LÉONIDE BOURGES
RUE DE LA BOURGOGNE
RUE DE ZUNDERT
RUE DES FLEURS
RUE CARNOT
RUE FRÉDÉRIC
FRANÇOIS MITTERRAND
DU PARC
RUE DU RÉSERVOIR
RUE BOUCHER
RUE ÉMILE BOGGIO
RUE EUGÈNE LEFEBVRE
RUE FRANÇOIS
CHEMIN DE LA LONGUE RUE
SENTIER DIT ST-MARTIN
RUE DU DOCTEUR GACHET
RUE FRANÇOIS VILLON
RUE DES AUNAIES
RUE ROGER TAGLIANA
RUE LOUIS GANNE

SIGHTS & ATTRACTIONS

Château d'Auvers

An excellent introduction to the Impressionist period in Auvers is the Château d'Auvers' audio-visual romp through the world of such artists as Daubigny, Pissarro, Cézanne and Renoir. ⓐ rue de Léry ⓣ 01 34 48 48 45 ⓦ www.chateau-auvers.fr ⓛ 10.30–18.00 Tues–Fri, until 18.30 Sat & Sun (summer); 10.30–16.30 Tues–Fri, until 17.30 Sat & Sun (winter)

L'Église d'Auvers

Perhaps the most poignant sight for many visitors is the church here. The delightful painting of it, *L'Église d'Auvers*, framed by a vibrant blue sky, now hangs in the Musée d'Orsay in Paris. The Romano-Gothic church is topped by a bell tower.

Maison de Van Gogh

Van Gogh lived his final days in a tiny attic room in the Auberge Ravoux, also called the Maison de Van Gogh. The room, sparse and emotive, with a tiny skylight, has been preserved as it was when Van Gogh died. One gets a sense of the despair that the artist felt towards the end, evident in such paintings as *Wheatfield with Crows*. Yet he produced many cheerful and vibrant works, such as the *Escalier d'Auvers*, a delightful scene of a staircase at the top of rue de la Sansonne.

Van Gogh produced many other famous and important works in Auvers, such as his self-portrait and the *Portrait of Dr Gachet*, which now hang in the Musée d'Orsay (see page 109). The Van Gogh Institute is determined to return his Auvers canvases to the room where he lived. ⓐ pl. de la Mairie ⓣ 01 30 36 60 60 ⓛ 10.00–18.00 Tues–Sun

Musée de l'Absinthe (Absinthe Museum)

A heady influence on many artists, including Van Gogh, was absinthe, a potent aperitif that preceded today's aniseed drink. The cloudy green beverage could be ruinous, as many lithographs and posters in this excellent museum show. ❸ 44 rue Alphonse Callé ❶ 01 30 36 83 26 ❶ 14.00–18.00 Sat, Sun & holidays (year round); also 14.00–18.00 Wed–Fri, June– Sept

▲ The beautiful l'Église d'Auvers inspired Vincent Van Gogh

AUVERS' OTHER FAMOUS ARTIST

Although Auvers will always be synonymous with Van Gogh, the village was also the adopted home of another significant 19th-century painter, Charles-François Daubigny. Daubigny found fame as an alumnus of the 'Barbizon school', whose members focused on the subject of nature; thus it was that he came to Auvers to paint the river Oise. The surrounding areas also inspired him, and while he lived here he produced works such as *Andrsy sur Oise* (1868), works that subsequently influenced the Impressionists.

Though in no sense a posthumous superstar like Van Gogh, Daubigny achieved far more recognition in his lifetime than Vincent did in his. The Atelier de Daubigny is a museum dedicated to his life and work.

Atelier de Daubigny ⓐ 61 rue de Daubigny ⓣ 01 34 48 03 03 ⓛ 14.00–18.30 Thur–Sun

RETAIL THERAPY

Auvers Tourist Office Lots of art books and postcards, but also little art trinkets, such as painters'-palette earrings. Contact details on page 122.

Un Certain Regard Art and craftwork gallery with art books and original works by 13 local artists. Friendly, original and agreeable, even if you don't buy anything. ⓐ 2 rue Montmaur ⓣ 06 71 17 06 13 ⓛ 09.30–18.00, closed Mon afternoon

Galerie d'Art Contemporain This contemporary art gallery holds exhibitions of artists' work and sells reproductions of Van Gogh works as well as original works of contemporary amateur artists.
ⓐ 5 rue Montcel ⓣ 01 34 48 00 10 ⓦ www.auversomc.com
ⓛ 10.00–16.00 Tues–Sun

TAKING A BREAK

Au Verre Placide £ ❶ A relaxing place to have a sandwich made with hearty country bread, a drink or light meal (by menu or à la carte). The local artists' work that adorns the walls is for sale.
ⓐ 20 rue du General de Gaulle ⓣ 01 34 48 02 11 ⓛ 12.00–15.00 & 19.30–23.00 Thur–Tues

Le Chemin des Peintres £ ❷ Located in an 1848 building, this charming restaurant/tea salon serves both traditional and modern cuisine made from local farm produce. ⓐ 3 bis rue de Paris
ⓣ 01 30 36 14 15 ⓛ Lunch, dinner tea salon 11.00–17.00 weekdays, until midnight Sat & 19.00 Sun

Auberge Ravoux £–££ ❸ An artists' café since 1876, this cosy restaurant in the Maison de Van Gogh serves such treats as *Gigot de Sept Heures* (lamb), the house speciality. ⓐ 8 rue de la Sansonne
ⓣ 01 30 36 60 60 ⓛ Lunch 12.00–16.00, Tea salon 16.00–18.00, closed Mon, Tues & Nov–end Feb

Reims

Reims (pronounced 'Rhants'), 143 km (89 miles) northeast of Paris
in the heart of champagne country, is a magnet for lovers of the
bubbly stuff.

This area is also known for its tumultuous history,
gentle countryside and one of Europe's finest Gothic cathedrals.
The 'Coronation Capital of France' is a city of ancient abbeys and
modern factories, art museums, cobbled squares and modern,
red-brick areas. Set among the extensive hills of vineyards, atop
some 250 km (155 miles) of chalk caves storing millions of bottles
of aging effervescent wine, Reims is an attractive city well worth
at least a day trip from Paris.

Europe's northernmost grape-growing area is a pleasant train
ride from the French capital. The first sign of champagne country
comes just outside the town of Epernay, where the grand buildings
of some venerable champagne houses, like ornate railway stations,
are seen to the right. Soon after come vineyards planted with
orderly rows of grapes.

Day tickets for buses within Reims are €2.50 and include
the airport shuttle. With these, it is easy to get around to some
of the champagne houses a few blocks from the city centre,
although it is also possible to walk to some with a map from
the tourist board.

Comité Régional du Tourisme

Ⓦ www.tourisme-champagne-ardenne.com

Reims Tourist Board ⓐ 2 rue Guillaume de Machault (beside the
cathedral) ⓣ 03 26 77 45 00 Ⓦ www.reims-tourisme.com

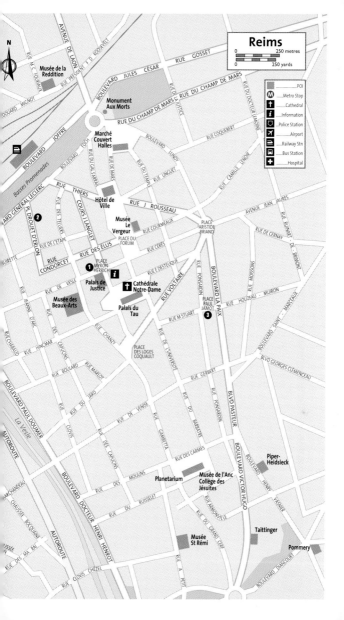

GETTING THERE

Trains for the one-and-three-quarter-hour trip to Reims depart from Paris several times a day from Gare de l'Est, so it is possible to leave in the morning, visit the city and several caves or vineyards, and be back in Paris by late evening especially now thanks to the

REIMS' CROWNING GLORY

The **Cathédrale Notre-Dame**, which is every bit the equal of its Parisian namesake, is of great interest both historically and architecturally. UNESCO has gone so far as to call it 'one of the masterpieces of Gothic art', and it is certainly rich in ornamentation, with some 2,300 statues decorating the exterior. The interior has high arches and vaults with magnificent stained-glass windows at each end. At the south end, modern windows by Marc Chagall depict biblical scenes. The rose windows at the north end are even more impressive and ornate.

To the considerable amount of French people who still consider themselves monarchists, the cathedral has enormous resonance: starting with Clovis in 496, the country's monarchs were crowned on this site (the present structure was started in 1211 but was preceded by at least one other building). The coronation of Charles VII here in 1429 is particularly interesting as we know that Joan of Arc was present. Indeed, Charles was a key figure in the 17-year-old's campaign to rid this part of France of British and Burgundian domination. ◐ 07.30–19.30 daily, free entrance, with (paying) guided visits in English and a visit to the towers.

Cathédrale Notre-Dame up close and personal

TGV (45 minutes). Costs vary depending on the time of day and week. For details, visit Ⓦ www.sncf-voyages.com

By car from Paris to Reims is 144 km (90 miles), around one and a half hours, via the A4.

SIGHTS & ATTRACTIONS

If a pleasant stroll is what you're after, then from the train station, place Drouet d'Erlon, a charming pedestrian street lined with hotels, bars, several Irish pubs and shops, leads into the city centre. A number of Roman remnants are on show right in the city, namely the Porte de Mars, enormous Roman arches dating from the year 200, and the place du Forum, a long semi-underground Roman gallery.

Cellar tours

Reims was built on bubbles and its major attraction remains champagne. The best way to appreciate it is through a tour of the cellars. More than a dozen of the famous houses offer tours, with rates averaging about €7. These are a bargain, as the price usually includes one or two glasses of champagne, which cost about €6 each at local bars.

Guides lead tours deep into the chalk cellars, 15–25 m (49–82 ft) underground. These Roman quarries, abandoned since the 3rd century BC, were excavated to get stone for building. The subterranean labyrinths of cool caves were only later used for champagne-making and storage. Down in the dimly lit caverns stand row upon row of dusty champagne bottles going through the second fermentation.

Guides explain, step by step, the complex process of producing a bottle of bubbly, from picking to fermenting to blending, the second fermentation, *remuage* (turning the bottles to collect the sediment) and *dégorgement* (removing the sediment). They impart a real sense of the pride the great houses take in producing their fine champagnes.

Tours end in the tasting room, with a glass or two of the house's fine champagne to sample. There, oenologists may explain that the effervescent beverage is best sipped from tall tulip or flute glasses, which focus the tiny, perfect bubbles in continuous streams, rather than broad, fishbowl glasses which dissipate bubbles and aroma.

Taittinger, a relatively young house but with ancient cellars, provides one of the best tours. It starts with a short film in a screening room with large murals explaining the wine-making process. An extensive, one-hour tour with knowledgeable guides follows. The cellars have some ancient abbey doors and a statue of St John the Baptist, the patron saint of cellar workers. 🄰 9 pl. St-Nicaise 🄣 03 26 85 84 33 🄦 www.taittinger.com

Nearby, the **Pommery** house is in the most impressive building, like a castle. Its traditional tour through part of its 18 km (11 miles) of cellars ends in a huge tasting room featuring an enormous carved barrel end, and massive barrels. 🄰 5 pl. du Général Gourand 🄣 03 26 61 62 56 🄦 www.pommery.com

In the **Piper-Heidsieck** (pronounced 'peeper') tours, a little automated amusement-ride car runs along tracks through the cellar with a taped announcement, all to dramatic organ music. The cars pass bunches of concrete stone grapes, the size of beach balls, hanging from the walls, giant hands holding grapes, and statues of men doing the turning. It is more like a theme park than an authentic champagne cellar. 🄰 51 blvd Henry Vasnier 🄣 03 26 84 43 44 🄦 www.piper-heidsieck.com 🄘 no visits in Jan &Feb

Details on all champagne houses are to be found at Ⓦ www.umc.fr. The tourist office has information on all champagne tours and the addresses of the cellars. Some tours are by appointment only or for groups. Others have regular tours and it is just a matter of showing up.

Hot-air ballooning

If you want to get really high on the champagne region, take a hot-air balloon ride. Inflated balloons carrying four or five passengers lift gently away, over the slopes, where grapes grow in patterned fields, the rows as orderly as bottles in the long cellars. The trip ends, appropriately enough, with ground crew waiting with fluted glasses, silver ice buckets and bottles of chilled *grand cru*. The local tourist office has information on hot-air balloon flights, which cost about £100 a person.

Vineyard tours

Outside of the cellars, there are above-ground tours of the earlier part of the process – the growing and harvesting of grapes from Reims. Minibuses follow the official Route du Champagne tourist trail through the vineyards and past ancient villages. Some go to the quaint village of Hautvillers, and the old abbey of Hautvillers where Dom Perignon lived and discovered how to put the fizz into the wine. Part of the abbey, greatly damaged during the French Revolution, is now a champagne museum. Various tableaux depict how the innovative monk first stopped the bottles with cork (an idea from Spanish monks) and how he gave them their distinctive, long-necked shape.

● *Local produce in Reims*

A typical vineyard tour for groups of two to eight people, in a minibus, is €20 per person. They depart from Epernay Tourist Office at 09.30 or 14.30 according to the season. You can also choose a guided tour by bike or on foot (bike rental is €10 at the start of the trip). Call before you go, to make sure the site is open. ⓐ 11 rue du Bas, 51530 Mancy ① 03 26 59 45 85 ⓦ www.champagne-domimoreau.com

RETAIL THERAPY

Souvenir shops in the tourist information office and local stores sell boxes of St Rémi Galettes (cookies; €2.50 a box of 12); sandstone gargoyle replicas of the ones on the cathedral for €37 and other sandstone carvings of vineyard workers for about €55. All the champagne houses have shops selling their products.

La Boutique Champenoise On the square facing the cathedral, this wine store has 500 different types of champagne, so you'll easily be able to find something to suit your taste and your budget. ⓐ 6 pl. du Cardinal Luçon ① 03 26 40 12 12

Caves des Sacres Right next door to La Boutique Champenoise, this has a wide range of souvenirs, from postcards and fridge magnets to fine, locally made tapestries. This is a great place for champagne paraphernalia, such as elegant glass flutes with holders and silver-plated ice buckets. You can also buy local products like jars of mustard and local vinegars. ⓐ 5 pl. du Cardinal Luçon ① 03 26 47 35 89

◗ *Boutique Champenoise, a champagne-lover's paradise*

TAKING A BREAK

Café du Palais £ ❶ While this atmospheric café may be popular with tourists, by far the greatest number of clientele is local. Very good, friendly service accompanies the excellent wine list and fine family food (mum cooks the main courses, daughter the sweets, and the son manages the front). ❸ 14 pl. Myron-Herrich ❶ 03 26 47 52 54 ⓦ www.cafedupalais.fr ❶ Lunch only, as the café closes at 21.00

Le Grand Café £ ❷ With its wood and mirrors, paintings and old black-and-white photographs of France, this café is a visual treat. The speciality of the house is *moules frites* (mussels with chips) served non-stop and champagne. ❸ 92 pl. Drouet d'Erlon ❶ 03 26 47 61 50

Le Vigneron £ ❸ The wine-maker restaurant is like a wine museum with thematic wall posters, wicker grape baskets, ploughs, wine kegs, line drawings and cartoons of champagne subjects. All this with fine food and service. Try the local aperitif Ratafia (fortified red wine with oranges) and *feuilles de vigne farcies* (stuffed vine leaves). ❸ pl. Paul Jamot ❶ 03 26 79 86 86

● *Follow the signs*

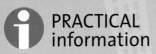

PRACTICAL
information

Directory

GETTING THERE
By air

Eight major airlines fly to France from 14 gateways. New budget airlines connect several secondary UK destinations to the French capital. The two major international airports in Paris are Roissy-Charles de Gaulle (handling most international flights) and Orly (most domestic and some European routes), while Beauvais specialises in charter flights.

Orly (ORY) ❶ 08 92 68 15 15 (06.00–23.45; €0.34/min) Ⓦ www.adp.fr

Paris-Beauvais (BVA) ❶ 08 92 68 20 66 or 08 92 68 20 73 (08.00–22.30; €0.37/min) Ⓦ www.aeroportbeauvais.com

Roissy-Charles de Gaulle (CDG) ❶ 08 92 68 15 15 (€0.34/min) Ⓦ www.adp.fr

Air Canada ❶ 0825 880 881 Ⓦ aircanada.com

Air France ❶ 36 54 Ⓦ airfrance.com

American Airlines ❶ 0 810 872 872 Ⓦ aa.com

British Airways ❶ 0 825 825 400 Ⓦ ba.com

Delta Airlines ❶ 0 811 640 005 Ⓦ delta.com

easyJet ❶ 08 25 08 25 08 Ⓦ easyjet.com

KLM/Northwest Airlines ❶ 0 890 710 710 Ⓦ nwa.com

RyanAir ❶ 08 92 68 20 73 Ⓦ ryanair.com

United ❶ 08 10 72 72 72 Ⓦ unitedairlines.co.uk

US Airways ❶ 08 10 63 22 22 Ⓦ usairways.com

Virgin ❶ 0 8 20 528 528 Ⓦ virgin.com

Many people are aware that air travel emits CO_2, which contributes to climate change. You may be interested in the possibility of lessening the environmental impact of your flight through the charity Climate Care, which offsets your CO_2 by funding environmental projects around the world. Visit Ⓦ www.climatecare.org

By rail

The Eurostar provides fast, seamless connections from London's St Pancras International station to central Paris (Gare du Nord) in two-and-a-half hours. By booking two months or more in advance, you can get great savings, and travel mid-week is cheaper than on weekends. Ⓦ www.eurostar.com

The Thalys high-speed train links Paris to Brussels and Amsterdam. Ⓦ www.thalys.com

For information and tickets for all rail travel (including high-speed trains called TGV) in France and Europe, contact the SNCF or visit one of their offices in Paris. ☎ 08 92 35 35 35 Ⓦ www.voyages-sncf.com

🔺 *Travel in style*

By road

Travelling by car from Calais to Paris, the 289 km (179 miles) takes just under three hours. Take the N1 south. Depending on where you approach Paris from, you'll join the ring road at one of the 30 *portes* (gateways) that punctuate the 35 km (21 miles) of expressway. Based on the area you are heading towards, you have a choice between the *périphérique intérieur* (inner ring road), which runs in a clockwise direction, and the *périphérique extérieur* (outer ring road), which runs counter-clockwise.

Traffic flow and journey times between gateways are displayed on illuminated overhead panels. Exit signs for each gateway into the city are given plenty of time in advance, so you can make sure you get in the right-hand lane. The speed limit is 80 km/h (50 mph) on ring roads and 50 km/h (30 mph) in urban areas. Driving is on the right and seat belts are mandatory, in the back too.

Coaches depart every two days from May to the end of October, leaving from London. A one-way ticket costs £25. Ⓦ www.busabout.com Ⓦ www.eurolines.com has coaches driving year-round.

Paris has two-way coach links with all major mainland European cities.

By water

There are many connections from Britain to France by sea. For information on the main ferry services, see Ⓦ www.directferries.co.uk, Ⓦ www.condorferries.co.uk, Ⓦ www.aferry.co.uk, Ⓦ www.brittany-ferries.co.uk

ENTRY FORMALITIES

Citizens of EU countries need only a current valid identity card to enter France, but should bring their passports as well. Citizens of

Australia, Canada, Finland, New Zealand, Norway, Sweden and the US need a passport but can stay for up to 90 days without a visa. South Africans need a tourist visa. Contact the Consulat Général de France in Johannesburg (❸ PO Box 1027 Parklands 2101) or Visa Services (ⓐ 191 Jan Smuts Av., 3rd floor, Standard Bank Building, Rosebank 2196 ❶ (27) 11 778 56 02 ⓦ www.consulfrance-jhb.org). All other passport holders should check with their nearest French embassy or consulate. For more information, see ⓦ www.diplomatie.gouv.fr

Visitors may bring in personal possessions and goods for personal use. The Single European Market allows visitors to bring in and take out most things as long as taxes have been paid on them in an EU country and they are for personal consumption. For more information, contact ⓦ www.douane.gouv.fr

MONEY

The euro is the currency of France and many other countries in the EU. €1 is divided into 100 cents. Notes come in €5, €10, €20, €50, €100, €200 and €500. Coins come in €1 and €2 and in 1, 2, 5, 10, 20 and 50 cents.

Bureaux de change, available at train stations, airports and main bank branches, are usually open late. Check buying/selling exchange rates and commission charged by agencies before using their service. If you have an international credit or debit card, automatic teller machines (ATMs) are widely available and most have service in English. By far the majority of travellers today use ATMs, the most economical system. Credit cards are widely accepted, particularly Visa and MasterCard.

The following numbers may be useful if you lose your credit cards:

American Express ❶ 01 47 77 72 00
Carte Bleue/Visa ❶ 0 825 00 91 19
Diner's Club ❶ 08 10 31 41 59

Eurocard/MasterCard ☎ 01 45 67 84 84
JCB ☎ 01 42 86 06 01

HEALTH, SAFETY & CRIME

There are no special food and drink precautions to take. Tap water is drinkable, unless otherwise marked. France is famous for its excellent health care, and the European Health Insurance Card entitles citizens from EU countries to the state-funded health-care scheme in France or other EU countries in which they are staying. (For more information in Britain, see Ⓦ www.direct.gov.uk.) For non-EU travellers, however, it can be expensive, so you should purchase your own health insurance before travelling.

In an emergency, call SAMU (dial 15), the emergency ambulance service. Aspirin and other basic medicines are available at pharmacies (indicated with a green cross), many of which are open on Sundays.

Violent crime is rare in the city centre and around the major tourist sights, although some of the *banlieues* (suburbs) are not safe after dark. However, pickpocketing is widespread, especially on the metro and other public transport, at major tourist sights and even in museums, so keep your bags and wallets closed and well out of reach, and be vigilant. Backpacks, particularly their front-zippered pockets, are a common target for pickpockets, so don't keep anything valuable in those, unless you carry them in front of you.

Valuables, including important documents, should be left in your hotel safe if possible. Avoid carrying large cameras and purses and other things that will make you a tourist target.

Pedestrians should be extremely careful when crossing the road; watch out for cars, motorbikes, scooters and even rollerbladers, as the average Parisian tends to take liberties where road safety is concerned. Look both ways before crossing, and make sure you respect the zebra crossings and traffic lights, as some drivers won't. Parisians of all ages seem to enjoy the thrill of dashing across at the last second; you may not want to do the same.

Hostess bars, particularly in the Pigalle neighbourhood, can charge exorbitant prices, so beware.

If you do require assistance, police are fairly obvious in dark-blue uniforms with the word 'police' prominently displayed. They are quite helpful, although most do not speak much English.

OPENING HOURS

Most services, shops and businesses are open all day from 09.00 or 09.30 to 18.00 or 19.00. Major department stores usually stay open late one night per week. Smaller boutiques often open later in the mornings, at around 10.00 or 11.00. On Sunday, most shops and businesses are closed, although Sunday shopping is prevalent in the Marais district and around the quays of Canal St-Martin.

Banking hours are usually 09.00–16.30 on weekdays, though some banks are open on Saturday.

Most museums are closed either Monday or Tuesday, but the larger ones have at least one night per week when they'll stay open until around 22.00.

TOILETS

Some public toilets, which are usually quite clean, can be found in Paris. They are supervised and cost around €0.40, closing in the evenings. Coin-operated 'superloos' are available for free and are automatically cleaned after each visitor. While cafés do not usually welcome people using their toilets unless they are paying customers, some don't mind and have coin entry (usually €0.20). Some toilets are unisex. Department stores offer free toilet facilities. Shopping centres and arcades also usually have toilets, some free, some not. You have to pay to go to the toilets in railway stations, but they are free at the airports. You will also find supervised toilets in most of the large parks and gardens in the city.

CHILDREN

Paris is child-friendly, and children are welcome in restaurants (although not as much as dogs!). Getting around by metro can be tiring for young children, however, as there are a lot of climbs and long walks in the stations. This can also be hard for parents with buggies. Baby food and nappies are available in supermarkets throughout the city.

Attractions and activities especially suitable for children can be found at ⓦ www.parisinfo.com. Some of the best are:

- **Bois de Vincennes** The Ferme de Paris is a farm in the east side of this area in the 12th *arrondissement*, featuring farm animals and a vegetable garden tended by children. From 31 May to 13 Sept, kids can enjoy '*Pestacles*' (music festivals for children) in the wood's Parc Floral.

- **Cité des Enfants** This attraction at La Villette (northeast, in the 19th) is full of interactive learning activities for youngsters aged 3 to 12. For contact details, see Cité des Sciences (see page 89).

- **Disneyland Resort Paris** This is probably the biggest attraction for most kids, and is accessible by RER A east to Marne-la-Vallée-Chessy. ❶ 01 60 30 60 53 ⓦ www.disneylandparis.com ⏱ 10.00–20.00 Mon–Fri, 09.00–20.00 Sat & Sun, until 23.00 in summer (check internet for details).

- **La Ferme de Paris** ⓐ route de Pesage, Bois de Vincennes, 12th
  ① 01 43 28 47 63 ⓛ 13.30–18.30 Teus–Sun (school holidays);
  13.30–18.30 weekends & public holidays (summer, until 17.00
  winter) Ⓝ RER C Joinville le Pont

- **Jardin d'Acclimatation** This park in the Bois de Boulogne (west
  side) includes an old-fashioned puppet theatre, miniature train,
  merry-go-round and Exploradôme, with arts and science exhibits.
  ⓐ Bois de Boulogne, 16th ① 01 40 67 90 82 ⓛ 10.00–18.00,
  until 19.00 May–Sept Ⓝ Metro: Sablons

🔺 *Paris is a particularly child-friendly city*

- **Jardin du Luxembourg** With its small boat rentals and ornamental pond, puppet theatre and pony rides, this garden is always a good choice. For more details, see page 100.

- **Palais de la Découverte (Palace of Discovery)** Kids can enjoy interactive exhibits here, including those in astronomy and earth sciences. 🅰 av. Franklin Roosevelt, 8th 🕿 01 56 43 20 21 🅦 www.palais-decouverte.fr 🕐 09.30–18.00 Tues–Sat, 10.00–19.00 Sun Ⓜ Metro: Champs-Élysées Clémenceau

COMMUNICATIONS
Internet
There is free internet access in all the main train stations, and cyber cafés are plentiful, especially in the city centre. Most cafés have a large @ in the name. If you need help navigating the French AZERTY keyboard, staff usually speak some English. A popular chain is called Milk because they serve milkshakes; there are several locations throughout Paris.

Milk 🅰 110 blvd Saint-Germain (7th) & 31 blvd Sebastopol (3rd) 🕿 08 2000 1000 🅦 www.milklub.com for other locations 🕐 24 hours

Another option is using the free Wi-Fi connection offered by the Paris town hall available in many public squares from 09.00 to 23.00. Just look for people tapping laptops. Many regular cafés offer this service now, as well as fast-food joints Quick and McDonald's.

Phone
Télécartes (telephone cards) in two sizes (50 units for €6 and 120 units for €15) are on sale at *tabacs* (tobacco stores), news-stands and main metro and RER stations. Public phones are found in post offices, railway

and metro stations and in the street, and in some bars and restaurants. They generally take telephone cards and credit cards.

As in the rest of Europe, all GSM-compatible mobile phones should be useable in France. You can get a French telephone number at any telecom shop if you want to avoid being charged international rates but want to retain your current operator. Otherwise you can sign up with one of the French operators – Orange, SFR or Bouygues Télécom

TELEPHONING FRANCE

To telephone France from abroad, dial the international code first (usually 00), then 33 and the number (skipping the first '0'). All numbers in France have ten digits and start with 0. In Paris, they start with 01.

TELEPHONING ABROAD

To make an international call from France, dial 00 first, then the country code, followed by the local area code and the number.
Country codes:

Australia 61
Canada 1
New Zealand 64
Republic of Ireland 353
South Africa 27
UK 44
USA 1

International operator 32 12
French directory 12

– but be aware that they will often try to lock you into long-term contracts. You can also rent cellphones, a good choice being **Cellhire** (🅰 182 av. Charles de Gaulle, 92522 Neuilly sur Seine 📞 01 41 43 79 40 🌐 www.cellhire.fr).

Post

The French postal service is reliable and efficient. The main post office, located at 52 rue du Louvre, is open 24 hours a day, though service is limited after 19.00. For *poste restante* service, letters should be addressed (preferably with the surname underlined and in capitals) to Poste Restante, 52 rue du Louvre, 75001 Paris (📞 01 40 28 76 00). Other post offices are open 08.00–19.00 Monday to Friday and 08.00–12.00 on Saturday.

Stamps are for sale in self-service machines in the post offices as well as *tabacs* (tobacco stores). Postboxes are yellow. Stamps for letters and cards up to 20 grams cost €0.60 within Europe and €0.90 to North America, Australia and New Zealand.

ELECTRICITY

Electricity is 220 volts, 50 Hz, with round-pin wall sockets. UK or non-EU visitors bringing in appliances will need an adaptor, and North Americans will need a transformer as well.

TRAVELLERS WITH DISABILITIES

Paris is making a concerted effort to assist those with disabilities. The '*Tourisme & Handicap*' label on cultural and leisure sights shows access and facilities for one or more categories of disability. Some restaurants and hotels are also posting the same label. For more information see the Paris Visitors Bureau website at 🌐 www.paris.info.com

A number of buses accommodate wheelchairs, and the RER A and metro line 14 have lifts for those with limited mobility. The rest of the metro system is not yet wheelchair-friendly. The RATP (municipal transport system) issues transport network maps that show the bus routes that accommodate wheelchairs. The RER also has special ramps that can be fitted at doorways for wheelchairs. For more information, contact ⓦ www.infomobi.com or call ☎ 08 10 64 64 64

The **Compagnons du Voyage** (☎ 01 53 11 11 12), a private association, provides travel companions and works with the RATP/SNCF to enable handicapped travellers to be accompanied on the metro, RER, bus and trains (in the whole Île-de-France region). This service costs €25 per hour in the Parisian area Monday to Saturday and €37.50 on Saturdays, Sundays and public holidays.

For blind people or the visually impaired, the **AVH** (Association Valentine Haüy ⓐ 5 rue Duroc, 7th ☎ 01 44 49 27 27 ⓦ www.avh.asso.fr) is a good contact.

For information on transport in special vehicles for wheelchairs, contact the following companies and associations:

AIHROP Prices vary, depending on the length of voyage.
☎ 01 41 29 01 29

ASA The charge is €20 for a one-way trip, plus €5 for the accompanying personnel. ☎ 01 42 03 61 67

TOURIST INFORMATION

Paris Convention and Visitors Bureau, Main Welcome Centre

ⓐ 25 rue des Pyramides, 1st ☎ 08 92 68 30 00 (€0.34/min)
ⓦ www.parisinfo.com ⓛ 10.00–19.00 Jun–Oct; 10.00–19.00 Mon–Sat, 11.00–19.00 Sun & holidays Nov–May ⓜ Metro: Pyramides

Other welcome centres, with the same telephone number and website, are to be found throughout Paris at the following addresses:

Anvers Welcome Centre ⓐ facing 72 blvd Rochechouart, 9th
🕐 10.00–18.00 (except 25 Dec, 1 Jan & 1 May) Ⓝ Metro: Anvers
Carrousel du Louvre Welcome Centre ⓐ pl. de la Pyramide Inversée,
99 rue de Rivoli, 1st 🕐 10.00–18.00 Ⓝ Metro: Palais Royal-Musée
du Louvre
Clemenceau Welcome Centre ⓐ av. Marigny/av. des
Champs-Élysées, 8th 🕐 09.00–19.00 (closed 14 Jul)
Ⓝ Metro: Champs-Élysées-Clémenceau
Expo/Porte de Versailles Welcome Centre ⓐ 1 pl. de la Porte de Versailles
🕐 11.00–19.00 during trade fairs Ⓝ Metro: Porte de Versailles
Gare de Lyon Welcome Centre ⓐ 20 blvd Diderot, 12th
Ⓝ 09.00–18.00 Mon–Sat (closed 1 May) Ⓝ Metro: Gare de Lyon
Gare du Nord Welcome Centre ⓐ 18 rue de Dunkerque, 9th
🕐 08.00–18.00 (closed 25 Dec, 1 Jan & 1 May) Ⓝ Metro: Gare du Nord
Montmartre Welcome Centre ⓐ 21 pl. du Tertre, 18th 🕐 10.00–19.00
Ⓝ Metro: Abbesses

BACKGROUND READING

Citizens by Simon Schama. Compelling account of how events
conspired to cause a ferocious revolution.
The Da Vinci Code by Dan Brown. This mega-selling thriller visits
some of Paris's major locations.
The Flaneur: A Stroll through the Paradoxes of Paris by Edmund
White. A walking tour of the city in the company of an original
and iconoclastic mind.
A Moveable Feast by Ernest Hemingway. The story of how Hemingway
became a writer is told against a backdrop of 1920s Paris and a cast
of legendary characters.
Murder in the Marais by Cara Black. A gripping World War II mystery
takes the reader on a tour of the colourful Marais.

Notre Dame de Paris by Victor Hugo. The original story of why Quasimodo got the hump.

Paris: Architecture, History, Art by Ian Littlewood. The best cultural study of the city.

Sixty Million Frenchmen Can't be Wrong by Jean-Benoît Nadeau and Julie Barlow. For once, a non-patronising attempt to identify the essence of what it is to be French.

Strolling along the banks of the Seine provides a unique perspective of Paris

Emergencies

The following are emergency numbers:

Emergency services ⓘ 112 (not for car break-downs)

Fire service ⓘ 18

Police ⓘ 17

SAMU (ambulance service) ⓘ 15

SOS Médécins (doctors) ⓘ 01 47 07 77 77

SOS Dentaire (dentists) ⓘ 01 43 37 51 00

Children's burns ⓘ 01 44 73 62 54

Adults' burns ⓘ 01 42 34 17 58

Poison Treatment Centre ⓘ 01 40 05 48 48

Sexually transmitted diseases (Bichat Hospital) ⓘ 01 40 78 26 00

MEDICAL SERVICES

The American Hospital in Paris provides an emergency service 24 hours a day, seven days a week. Patients are looked after by a bilingual team (French–English) who have access to specialists on call, covering more than 20 medical and surgical fields.

The American Hospital in Paris ⓐ 63 blvd Victor Hugo, Neuilly-sur-Seine ⓘ 01 46 41 25 25 ⓦ www.american-hospital.org ⓜ Metro: Anatole France or Pont de Levallois

24-hour Pharmacy ⓐ Les Champs, 84 av. des Champs-Élysées, 8th ⓘ 01 45 62 02 41 ⓜ Metro: Franklin D Roosevelt

POLICE

In case of attack or theft, report it to either the nearest police station or *gendarmerie* to where the attack was carried out.

Préfecture de police ⓐ 9 blvd du Palais, 1st ⓘ 01 53 71 53 71 or 01 40 79 71 57 ⓦ www.prefecture-police-paris.interieur.gouv.fr ⓜ Metro: Cité

USEFUL PHRASES

Help!	**Fire!**	**Stop!**
Au secours!	Au feu!	Stop!
Ossercoor!	*Oh fur!*	*Stop!*

Call an ambulance/a doctor/the police/the fire service!
Appelez une ambulance/un médecin/la police/les pompiers!
*Ahperleh ewn ahngbewlahngss/ang medesang/lah poleess/
leh pompeeyeh!*

Lost and found office Préfecture de police 🄰 36 rue des Morillons, 15th
☎ 08 21 00 25 25 Ⓜ Metro: Convention

EMBASSIES & CONSULATES

Australia 🄰 4 rue Jean Rey, 15th ☎ 01 40 59 33 00
Ⓜ Metro: Bir Hakeim

Canada 🄰 35 av. Montaigne, 8th ☎ 01 44 43 29 00
Ⓜ Metro: Alma Marceau

New Zealand 🄰 7 ter rue Léonard de Vinci, 16th ☎ 01 45 01 43 43
Ⓜ Metro: Victor Hugo

Republic of Ireland 🄰 4 rue Rude, 16th ☎ 01 44 17 67 00
Ⓜ Metro: Charles de Gaulle-Etoile or Argentine

South Africa 🄰 59 quai d'Orsay, 7th ☎ 01 53 59 23 23 Ⓜ Metro: Invalides

UK 🄰 35 rue du Faubourg Saint-Honoré, 8th ☎ 01 44 51 31 00
Ⓜ Metro: Madeleine or St-Lazare

US 🄰 2 av. Gabriel, 8th ☎ 01 43 12 22 22 Ⓜ Metro: Champs-Élysées
Clémenceau

WHAT'S IN YOUR GUIDEBOOK?

Independent authors Impartial up-to-date information from our travel experts who meticulously source local knowledge.

Experience Thomas Cook's 165 years in the travel industry and guidebook publishing enriches every word with expertise you can trust.

Travel know-how Contributions by thousands of staff around the globe, each one living and breathing travel.

Editors Travel-publishing professionals, pulling everything together to craft a perfect blend of words, pictures, maps and design.

You, the traveller We deliver a practical, no-nonsense approach to information, geared to how you really use it.

Editorial/project management: Lisa Plumridge
Copy editor: Paul Hines
Layout/DTP: Alison Rayner
Proofreader: Wendy Janes

The publishers would like to thank the following companies and
individuals for supplying the copyright photographs for this book:
BigStockPhoto.com (Elena Elisseeva, page 40–1; András Sipos, page 74;
Graça Victoria, page 92); Dreamstime.com (Elena Elisseeva, page 35;
Jan Kranendonk, page 96); Pierrick Hamonet, page 57; Christopher
Holt, page 42; iStockphoto.com (Frédéric de Bailliencourt, page 87;
Si Khanh Nguyen, page 65); Aude Pasquier, page 153; Julia Peslier,
page 13; Pictures Colour Library, pages 5, 7, 16, 69 & 110; Alison Rayner,
pages 29, 66 & 107; SXC.hu (Christophe Libert, page 101; Jan Tonellato,
pages 48–9); Garry Marchant, all others.

Send your thoughts to
books@thomascook.com

- Found a great bar, club, shop or must-see sight that we don't feature?
- Like to tip us off about any information that needs a little updating?
- Want to tell us what you love about this handy little guidebook and
  more importantly how we can make it even handier?

Then here's your chance to tell all! Send us ideas, discoveries and
recommendations today and then look out for your valuable input
in the next edition of this title.

Email the above address (stating the title) or write to:
CitySpots Project Editor, Thomas Cook Publishing, PO Box 227,
Coningsby Road, Peterborough PE3 8SB, UK.